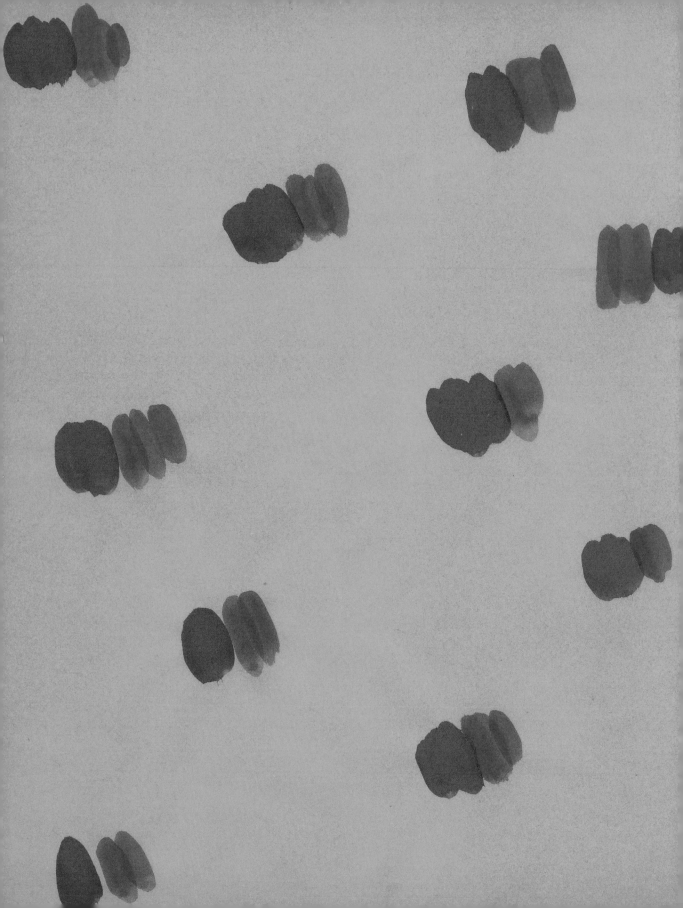

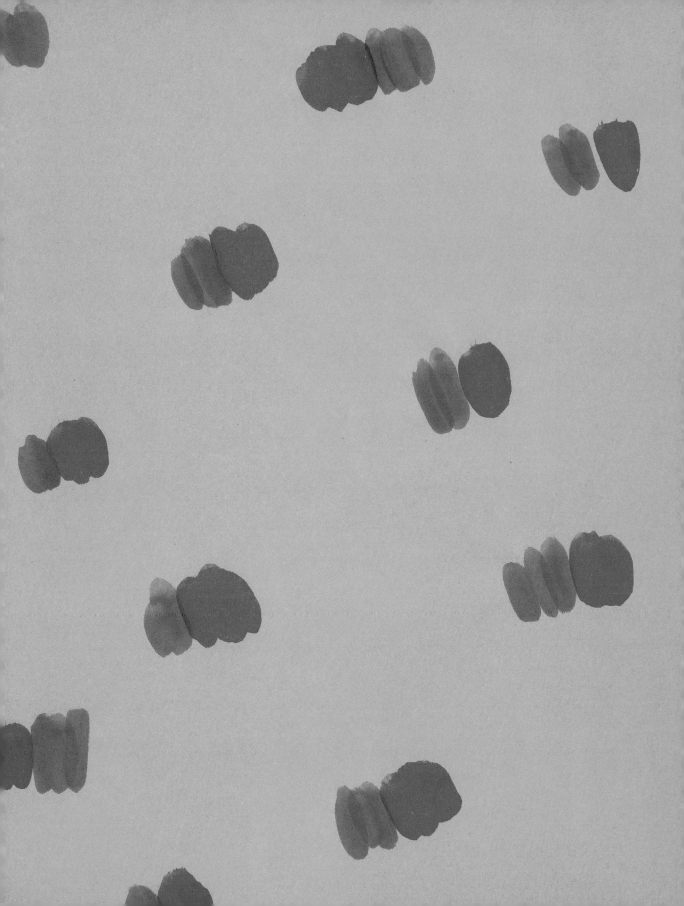

food + family

LUNCH LADY

AUD 19.95
USD 15.95
GBP 13.50
NZD 21.95

LUNCH LADY

food + family

AUD 19.95
USD 15.95
GBP 13.50
NZD 21.95

LUNCH LADY

food + family

LUNCH LADY

LUNCH LADY

AUD 19.95
USD 15.95
GBP 13.50
NZD 21.95

food + family

LUNCH LADY

Collect all editions
of the Lunch Lady
book series.

@hellolunchlady

growing babies organically.

Nature Baby provides a world that nurtures you, *your baby and nature*. All products are carefully selected for quality, purity and design and are produced in a way that cares for your baby, the earth and its workers. *Organic cotton* and *merino* are grown and processed without the use of harmful chemicals, leaving nothing on baby's clothes except *pure goodness*.

www.naturebaby.com

Jackson, 10 months, organic cotton bodysuit, triangle bib (navy foliage print). Nature Baby S/S17-18

LIGHTHOUSE
David Clapin

Our brand story starts in 1865 when Robert Harper started a trading company in his own name, specialising in tea, spices and flour. In 1891 he trademarked his business along with a drawing of a lighthouse with the word 'Lighthouse' written above it. Then in the early 1900s Robert Harper & Co. modernised the lighthouse symbol and gave it the name 'Empire Flour'. It remained this way for over 100 years. In 2002 the company was bought by Anchor Foods and returned to Western Australia. Almost instantly the word Empire was replaced with 'Lighthouse', inspired by the original trademarked logo. The Lighthouse symbol was first chosen as a metaphor for guidance and trust, 151 years later this still remains true.

TIGER TRIBE
Anthony Green

Our name has simple origins. From the beginning our business has focused on creating products that excite children's imaginations and tap into creative minds. It was important to find a name that embodied these ideals; one that parents and kids would have an immediate connection with. The tiger is such a vivid, dynamic and inspiring animal. It seemed the perfect choice. And here in Australia we often affectionately refer to kids as little tigers, so the double meaning was there too. And we're all looking for our tribe - a collective or group filled with like-minded folk. A place where we belong.

OBUS
Kylie Zerbst

Obus is the German word for Trolley Bus—the idea being that by wearing Obus, women of all ages could come onboard for an adventure. In my early twenties after studying and teaching design I took my first trip overseas to India and it changed my life. For someone who had barely travelled out of Victoria spending three months in India totally blew my mind. It changed the way I thought about things, the people around me, and how I wanted to spend my days. I decided I'd like to work in a more tactile way, to create things to wear, and that's when Obus was born. All these years later Obus is still on the road and travel has remained the central inspiration behind the way we work and what we create. Each collection we produce is inspired by a destination, and so, real or imagined we take our ladies on a different journey each season. Our summer collection 'Journey 42' takes us to Ukraine. Visit us at obus.com.au to view the collection.

THE HORSE
Scott + Amy Hawkes

We started in the shoe business so it was a play on a farrier shoeing horses. In the same way, we were shoeing people. We liked calling them leather saddles your feet carry. We think the name's got a bit of charm and heritage about it. We also wanted the name to have no real relationship to shoes. Fun fact—The Horse can also be rearranged to The Shoer.

RAINEBEAU
Sarah Fitzgerald

The name Rainebeau is a combination of two of our children's names, who are also great friends. We love the symbolism behind rainbows—they signify positivity, happiness, individuality and fun, which is what we're all about and what our lunchboxes are all about! We believe in the nutrition philosophy eat a rainbow because the vibrant colours in fruit and vegetables contain powerful health promoting nutrients. And we like to think our lunchbox design makes it easy to give children a rainbow for lunch every day.

HONEYBEE WRAP
Sherrie Adams

Our HoneyBee wraps are made from 100% organic cotton fabric, natural beeswax, jojoba oil, coconut oil and tree resin, so the name HoneyBee Wrap for our brand made sense. This collection of ingredients creates a flexible wrap that can be used over and over again. As a mother I was constantly looking for ways to reduce waste in our family and reduce the environmental impact we have on the earth. HoneyBee wrap was born from questioning how people stored food before plastic. I'm so happy to be able to provide a natural alternative to plastic for you and your family that is safe, non-toxic, eco friendly and compostable. The honeybee plays such a vital role on our planet but is currently in worldwide decline. To give bees a helping hand, you could plant a wild flower garden creating a bee hotel in your backyard. Bees are responsible for one third of what we eat, so we really need to look after them!

FLOW HIVE
Cedar Anderson

We invented a new way to harvest honey straight from a beehive, without disturbing the bees. You can watch the honey flow right from the hive and straight into the jar as the bees go about their business. There's something really fascinating about watching honey flow, it's still one of our favourite things to do. Beekeepers also talk about honey and nectar flows, meaning the times of year when lots of flowers are blooming and the bees are busy foraging. So the name Flow just seemed a natural fit. Over the last couple of years as thousands of people started keeping bees with our Flow system the name has taken on extra meaning for us. Because the flow on effect from these new beekeepers is amazing—we've heard from people turning entire neighbourhoods pesticide free and planting acres of wildflowers. That's something we are proud to be a part of.

HOMECAMP
Stephanie Francis

The Homecamp brand is all about utility partnered with a sense of style, we have a less is more functional kind of attitude, but always with good design in mind. We were looking for a simple and memorable name that also described this vibe and we think Homecamp sums it up perfectly. We're not really an extreme, conquer-the-elements type of outdoors brand. We want to encourage people into the outdoors but with some of the comforts of home. Homecamp reflects our laid back and relaxed attitude to enjoying nature and creating your own home out in the wild so you can stay a while.

NATURE BABY
Jacob Faull

Nature and Baby are synonymous with the idea of pure beginnings; to look after a baby you have to respect nature and to look after nature you have to bring your baby up with respect. The fonts we have chosen for our logo have the word baby as a fluid hand-made design and the word nature as a more structural and architectural font. We also have a little drawing of a baby, which stands strong but naked with the two. You could say we were trying to present an idea that was both strong yet vulnerable.

PROUD & PUNCH
Jess Virgin

From very early on, we knew exactly the kinds of ingredients and flavours we wanted to use in our products. The fruits and vegetables used in our Frozen Yoghurts and Juice Pops are sourced from Australian growers. The sugars in our Juice Pops come purely from the fruits; and none of our products use any concentrates, artificial colours, flavours, or preservatives. With so many frozen treats on supermarket shelves that appear healthy (but in fact, are not) our brand name and our packaging needed to tell people very quickly just how serious we are! Our name is a play on the old saying "proud as punch". We're PROUD—because our flavours are made with pride. We're proudly Australian and proudly real. And we're PUNCH—because we're all about big, positive flavours that we've made with love, and they pack a punch!

Hey foundation partner! What's the story behind your brand name?

///

Recipes

Star Power Pizza - sweet potato, potatoes, feta, rosemary & maple syrup

Available in Coles & Woolworths

lighthousebaking.com.au

Play with your food.

Making pizza bases from scratch is basically play-dough, except you are highly encouraged to eat it afterwards.

Lighthouse Bread & Pizza flour gives you expert results everytime, so all you have to focus on is the fun stuff.

For baking recipes, inspiration and advice visit our website; lighthousebaking.com.au

LIGHTHOUSE

LEADING LIGHT IN BAKING

SINCE 1865

playgrounds

In a small town in North Wales, one of the most unusual playgrounds in the world is trying to change the way we think about play. Welcome to The Land.

For a film about children playing, *The Land*, Erin Davis's eye-opening documentary, is surprisingly anxiety-inducing. For The Land is not your average playground. Built in an abandoned lot in the middle of a working-class Welsh neighbourhood, The Land looks, at first glance, like a literal garbage dump. It's a landscape littered with mud, broken furniture, pallets, broken playground equipment, concrete cylinders, piles of timber, more mud, a punching bag, broken toys, old tyres, a couple of shipping containers, the shell of an old speedboat and, for some reason, an armless mannequin hanging from a tree. But then you look again and you see the children, seemingly unsupervised and covered in mud, running, climbing, breaking, building and laughing their way through these piles of detritus. For those of us used to the clean, clinical world of most playgrounds, it's a moment of high-end cognitive dissonance. Where are their parents? Someone's going to die! Is that child ... starting a fire? Yes. Yes they are.

Yet hidden behind its seemingly dangerous facade, The Land might hold the key to one of the most basic questions of childhood: What is play? And how can we ensure our kids get the most out of it?

***

For something so fundamental to the development of children, play holds a vexed position for the modern child. As a society, we've become suspicious of unstructured time and unstructured space. Safety is the overarching watchword and we fill our kids' days with enriching activities designed to best cultivate their blooming minds. Play has become something to be monitored and shaped, from the toys we give to the games we create.

Barbara Chancellor, a Melbourne-based play researcher and academic, thinks we're losing sight of the bigger picture. "Poor teachers and parents today are bombarded with all these things they need to be doing to ensure their child's development. But play itself, unadorned and uninterrupted, is just as important as any other activity." She laughs, "If you'd only just back off, they'd probably get a lot out of it."

So, why exactly is play so important? Chancellor puts it plainly: "Any benefit you are looking for, you will find it in play: resilience, academic achievement, better behaviour, physical health. But these are just Trojan horses that justify it in the eyes of parents. Play is simply what young children do. It's how they learn everything, really."

But we're only just realising how important play is for developing minds—and how wrong we often get it when we try to intervene. "Play seems like the easiest thing in the world," Chancellor explains, "but we're realising that the relationship between kids and play, and us and their play, is more complex than we once thought. The more we look into it and think about it and observe it, the more we realise we don't know." >>

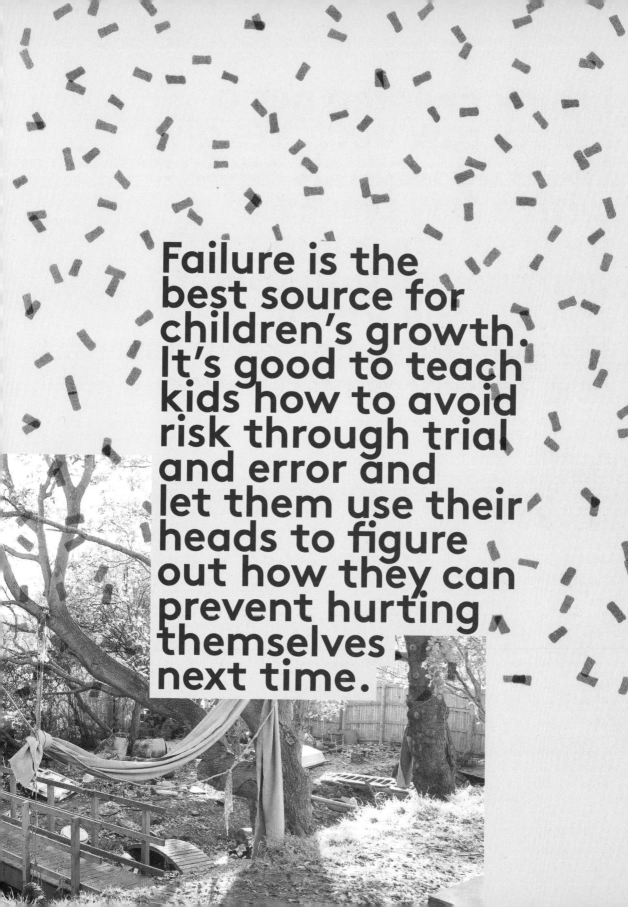

Failure is the best source for children's growth. It's good to teach kids how to avoid risk through trial and error and let them use their heads to figure out how they can prevent hurting themselves next time.

I think children get a pretty raw deal. We give them an asphalt square with a few pieces of mechanical equipment, and they're supposed to spend their imaginative life swinging backwards and forwards on a swing.

For Davis, coming to The Land was a revelatory moment in her understanding of what it meant for children to play. "You arrive and you think, Are these kids homeless? Is this a refugee camp? But the more and more time I spent there, I just realised that this place is poetry. It's living, breathing poetry. The very ground breathes and breeds playfulness."

Far from a negligence lawsuit waiting to happen, The Land is a particularly eye-catching example of the adventure playground movement. Developed from the ideas of the Danish landscape architect Carl Theodor Sørensen, adventure playgrounds eschew deliberate design and manufactured toys in favour of a ramshackle or junkyard aesthetic, filled with errata from the everyday. The emphasis is on unrestricted play, where children

are given the opportunity to become agents in their own story.

Sørensen opened the first adventure playground in Copenhagen in 1943, and the idea quickly spread around a post-war Europe that was poor in resources but rich in debris and junk. The concept made its way to England thanks to the efforts of a landscape architect named Marjory Allen. After seeing Sørensen's vision in action, she proposed that London's bomb sites could be converted into playgrounds. For the next thirty years, she became a tireless advocate for the free play of children, exemplified by her rallying cry, "Better a broken bone than a broken spirit." In one piece of archival footage, she explains her position: "I think children get a pretty raw deal. We give them an asphalt square with a few pieces of mechanical equipment, and they're supposed to spend their imaginative life swinging backwards and forwards on a swing."

Although no two adventure playgrounds are ever the same, they're all bound together by a sense of joyful chaos. These haven't been architecturally designed, or constructed from brand-new materials. They're built from recognisable, real objects cobbled together with varying degrees of success. There's old furniture, broken equipment and loose bits of wood. Paint or mud is daubed across most surfaces. Children, often filthy, hold and use tools, rarely in the way they're intended.

In many ways, these playgrounds hark back to an earlier, simpler time. "Forty years ago, back when I was teaching kinder," Chancellor tells me, "kids just played with old broken telephones, and plates, knives and forks. And then suddenly everything started being replaced with miniature plastic versions. But children are more than capable of playing with real stuff. They don't actually need pretend objects." At The Land, children can play with saws, hammers and lighters, and they do.

Of course, there is order to the seeming chaos. The very first bomb-site playgrounds were manned by "wardens", who doled out the tools and made sure things didn't get too out of hand. Over time these wardens evolved into playworkers, whose role is, more than anything, simply to watch and wait until they're needed. This is the core understanding of playwork: children can play perfectly well without our intervention. The job of the playworker is simply to do whatever they can to give a child control over their own story.

"The biggest thing that I took from my time at The Land," says Davis, "was that I learned to shut the hell up. I talk so much when I'm with kids. 'Oh wow, that's so interesting! How'd you do that?' Shut up already! It taught me to look to the child for a signal. Do they need me to be there? Do they need me to talk to them? Are they inviting me into this or do I just feel like I'm entitled to be part of it because I'm an adult?"

Not to say that playworkers are inactive. At The Land, every new shipment of junk is carefully appraised and scoured for hazards. "Risks and hazards are different things," explains one of the playworkers in the film. A risk is something that the child chooses to engage with, to appraise and work out. The playworker's job is to remove the hazards—jutting nails, unstable surfaces—that could cause children inadvertant harm and to offer gentle advice if it looks like things might be getting out of hand.

When you're watching Davis's film, it's hard not to feel a vertiginous lump in your throat as you watch a self-confident eleven-year-old climb eight metres up a tree, and then stride out onto an outstretched branch. A playworker watches it happen and offers a gentle suggestion when the boy gets to a thinner part of the branch. After a bit of banter, he backs off and then clambers down a nearby rope. It's a textbook playworker interaction: situation defused with the child still in control.

>>

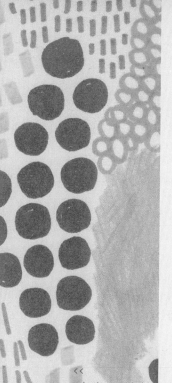

Kids who don't fight their own battles, or assess their own risks, never get the chance to form a sense of how they might one day navigate a world that's messy and confusing and full of unexpected terrors and joys.

<<

What's remarkable is that The Land suffers no more injuries than most regular playgrounds. Evidence suggests that when they're given responsibility for their own safety, children tend to take it. In his book *Messy*, the economist Tim Harford—profiled in our last issue—points out that for all the money spent on safety-proofing the modern playground, and there is a colossal amount of money spent, there's no real evidence that children are any safer or sustain fewer injuries. Indeed, a recent, broad-based study of supposedly 'risky' outdoor play—meaning activities involving great heights, high speeds, sharp tools, fire, water and fighting—showed that not only were there fewer injuries in the risky play, the children were also healthier, more social and less aggressive. In another study, a primary school in Auckland opened a junk-filled field for the kids to play in during recess. The result: fewer injuries, better classroom behaviour, increased academic engagement and the almost total disappearance of bullying.

Chancellor has seen these effects first-hand in her own research on Victoria's Bush Kinder programs, where children are given a period of time each week

to explore and play in bushland, without adult intervention. "After six months, we interviewed the teachers and parents and they all reported quite noticeable changes in their kids. They'd become much more observant and inquisitive. They'd calmed down, were less disruptive. It's difficult to make generalisations in academia, but I think the benefit of unstructured outside play is something you can pretty safely make generalisations about." Basically: let the children run, cuts and scrapes be damned.

Yet if there is one theme that ties together the experience of modern parenting, it is protectiveness. Not merely physical protectiveness, but also mental and emotional. It's hardwired into us. Kids are fragile and need to be protected until they can protect themselves. But kids who don't fight their own battles, or assess their own risks, or make their own play, never get the chance to form a sense of their own capacities and how they might one day navigate a world that's messy and confusing and full of unexpected terrors and joys.

"What I take away from playwork and apply to parenting is this idea of observing your child and then

responding to them, instead of always coming at them with your own fears or ideas," says Davis. "And that's hard, because you do want to be involved, and you do want to protect them, but it's like a muscle you need to build up. You see your child struggling with something. Are they reaching to you for help, or are they just trying to work it out on their own?"

She goes on: "We tend to see struggling as bad, or struggling as failure. But struggle is fascinating. It's how we work ourselves and the world out. Even in adulthood, reading a challenging novel, or going on a long hike, or doing a crossword is like a controlled struggle. It's our version of play. We should give our kids the opportunity to struggle as enjoyably as we do."

"The main thing we can do as adults is to make sure that children have time and space to play," Chancellor says. "Kids' play is so rich in imagination and story that it takes time to unfold. But these days kids don't get a lot of free time. It's not like it once was where you were chased out the back door and told to come back at dinner. Perhaps that's something we need to try and rediscover."

///

green

& PROUD OF IT

Oh yeah! It's not every day you find
a green, feel-good machine like this juicy number.
Get your dose of Paging Dr.Green at your
local supermarket.

PROUD & PUNCH™

FROZEN
YOGHURT

PROUDLY MADE
IN AUSTRALIA

fruity

&

PROUD OF IT

We're berry happy you've stumbled across our frozen Greek style yoghurt with Aussie grown berries. It's tart, tasty and waiting for you at your local supermarket.

PROUD
&
PUNCH™

the more the berrier

FROZEN GREEK STYLE YOGHURT
with RASPBERRY, BLUEBERRY & STRAWBERRY

500mL

beachy

keen

Healthy fish & veggie chips picnic (plus salads & mushy peas!)

POTATO SALAD WITH EGG, OLIVES + GREEN BEANS

- 1kg / 2.2lb baby potatoes
- sea salt, to taste
- big glug of olive oil
- 4 eggs, boiled and peeled
- 250g / 8.8oz green beans
- 100g / 3.5oz Ligurian olives, pitted
- handful of chives
- juice of 1 lemon

1. Preheat oven to 200°C / 400°F / Gas Mark 6.

2. Cut potatoes in half and place in baking tray with a big pinch of salt and a big glug of olive oil. Toss to coat and roast in oven until cooked through— about 20 minutes.

3. Meanwhile, top and tail beans and blanch them in boiling salted water for 3 minutes.

4. Drain beans and run cold water over them to prevent them from cooking further.

5. When potatoes are ready, remove them from oven.

6. Add beans, olives, chives and lemon juice to the tray, along with another big pinch of salt, and toss together.

7. Cut eggs in half and gently toss through.

8. Serve warm.

///

MUSHY PEAS

Serves 4

- 400g / 14oz peas, fresh or frozen
- 1 tbsp butter
- zest and juice of 1 lemon
- 1/4 cup mint, finely chopped

1. In a small saucepan, boil peas for about 4 minutes until they're really tender.

2. Drain peas and put them in a bowl with butter, zest, juice and mint.

3. Roughly mash peas with a potato masher or fork.

4. Season to taste and serve warm.

///

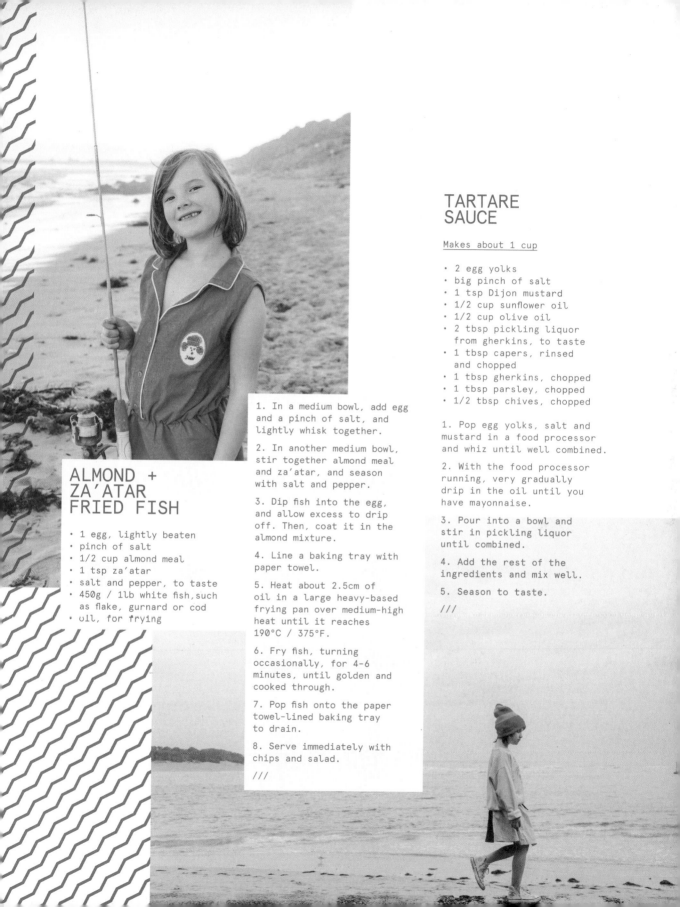

TARTARE SAUCE

Makes about 1 cup

- 2 egg yolks
- big pinch of salt
- 1 tsp Dijon mustard
- 1/2 cup sunflower oil
- 1/2 cup olive oil
- 2 tbsp pickling liquor from gherkins, to taste
- 1 tbsp capers, rinsed and chopped
- 1 tbsp gherkins, chopped
- 1 tbsp parsley, chopped
- 1/2 tbsp chives, chopped

1. Pop egg yolks, salt and mustard in a food processor and whiz until well combined.

2. With the food processor running, very gradually drip in the oil until you have mayonnaise.

3. Pour into a bowl and stir in pickling liquor until combined.

4. Add the rest of the ingredients and mix well.

5. Season to taste.

///

ALMOND + ZA'ATAR FRIED FISH

- 1 egg, lightly beaten
- pinch of salt
- 1/2 cup almond meal
- 1 tsp za'atar
- salt and pepper, to taste
- 450g / 1lb white fish, such as flake, gurnard or cod
- oil, for frying

1. In a medium bowl, add egg and a pinch of salt, and lightly whisk together.

2. In another medium bowl, stir together almond meal and za'atar, and season with salt and pepper.

3. Dip fish into the egg, and allow excess to drip off. Then, coat it in the almond mixture.

4. Line a baking tray with paper towel.

5. Heat about 2.5cm of oil in a large heavy-based frying pan over medium-high heat until it reaches 190°C / 375°F.

6. Fry fish, turning occasionally, for 4-6 minutes, until golden and cooked through.

7. Pop fish onto the paper towel-lined baking tray to drain.

8. Serve immediately with chips and salad.

///

CARROT FRIES

- 450g / 1lb carrots, chopped into fries
- 1 tbsp cornflour
- drizzle of olive oil
- 1 tsp thyme, finely chopped
- salt and pepper, to taste

1. Preheat oven to 200°C / 400°F / Gas Mark 6.

2. Pop carrot fries into a bowl with cornflour and a little salt and pepper, and toss to coat.

3. Drizzle with olive oil and toss.

4. Spread carrots in a single layer on a baking tray lined with baking paper, and bake for 40-45 minutes, turning halfway.

5. Toss thyme through cooked fries and serve immediately.

///

EGGPLANT CHIPS

- 2 medium eggplants
- 3 tbsp olive oil
- 1 garlic clove, crushed
- 1 tbsp rosemary, finely chopped

1. Slice eggplants into about 1/2cm pieces.

2. Lay eggplant pieces in a single layer on a baking tray lined with baking paper and sprinkle with salt. Leave for up to an hour to leach out water before baking.

3. Before baking, remove any excess water by dabbing eggplant pieces with some paper towel.

4. Preheat oven to 350°F / 175°C / Gas Mark 3.

5. In a small bowl, mix olive oil, garlic and rosemary.

6. Brush each eggplant piece with the oil mix and sprinkle with extra salt.

7. Place in the oven for 20-30 minutes. Remove any eggplant that cooks quicker, as the thinner bits can get a bit crispy.

8. Serve immediately.

///

POTATO CHIPS

- 1.5kg / 3.3lb potatoes
- drizzle of olive oil
- salt, to taste
- handful of rosemary sprigs

1. Preheat oven to 220°C / 425°F / Gas Mark 7.

2. Pop potatoes in a pot of boiling water for about 20-25 minutes.

3. Remove from heat, pour into a colander and run cold water over them to cool them enough to handle.

4. Chop potatoes into chip size.

5. Generously coat a baking dish with olive oil and place your chopped chips into it.

6. Sprinkle with salt and rosemary, and then glug on some more of the olive oil.

7. Pop in the oven for about 25 minutes. Give the tray a shake and toss the chips a few times throughout.

8. Once chips are crispy and golden, remove from oven and serve.

///

ROASTED GREEN BEANS

- 450g / 1lb fresh green beans
- drizzle of olive oil
- salt and pepper, to taste

1. Preheat oven to 220°F / 425°F / Gas Mark 7.

2. Pop green beans in a bowl and drizzle with olive oil. Toss to coat each bean.

3. Lay them on a baking tray, making sure they aren't touching, and sprinkle with salt and pepper.

4. Roast for 25-30 minutes, flipping once during cooking.

5. Serve immediately.

///

APPLE, FENNEL + RED CABBAGE SLAW

For the salad:

- 1/4 red cabbage
- 1 small fennel bulb
- 1 Granny Smith apple
- small handful of dill, very roughly chopped
- 1 bird's eye chilli, optional

For the dressing:

- 150ml / 5 fl oz buttermilk
- 1 tbsp apple cider vinegar
- 2 tbsp olive oil
- big pinch of salt

1. Using a mandolin, slice the cabbage into paper-thin shreds. Set aside into a large bowl.

2. Remove stalks from fennel and cut them in half, and then slice into paper-thin half-moons with a mandolin. Place in bowl with cabbage.

3. Slice apple into thin julienne batons (a mandolin with a julienne blade is best for this). Add to the bowl with the fennel and cabbage.

4. To make the dressing, place the dressing ingredients into a screw-top jar, and shake vigorously until combined.

5. Thinly slice the chilli, if using, and set aside.

6. Toss the coleslaw using your hands, and then pour the dressing over it. Toss again very gently, and then sprinkle chilli over the top.

7. Serve immediately.

///

MIXED GREENS GREEK SALAD

- 1/4 cup extra-virgin olive oil
- juice of 1/2 lemon
- 1 tbsp red wine vinegar
- salt and ground pepper, to taste
- 4 cups salad greens (spinach, baby gem lettuce, rocket, witlof and mizuna), rinsed and patted dry, then torn
- 2 tbsp fresh mint leaves, chopped
- 2 tbsp fresh oregano, chopped
- 1 cucumber, cut into ribbons
- 6 small ripe tomatoes, chopped
- 1/2 red onion, thinly sliced and separated into rings
- 1/4 cup kalamata olives
- 115g / 4oz Greek feta, crumbled

1. Combine olive oil, lemon juice, vinegar, salt and pepper in a salad bowl.

2. Add the salad greens, mint leaves, oregano, tomatoes, cucumber, red onion and olives.

3. Toss to mix well.

4. Sprinkle with feta before serving.

///

*shells bells

Dove Shells

Dove shells are world travellers, common in the tropics and more temperate parts of the Australian coast. They're also travellers on the eating front: Columbellidae, the family of snails who live in the shell, crawl on the hard undersides of rocks and even on seagrass beds, and like other molluscs, they eat both plant and animal matter, which is rare in the snail world. Dove shells vary wildly in shape—from short and stubby to long and delicate, smooth, knobby and multicoloured. On the Hawaiian island of Ni'ihau, you might find local, colourful dove shells strung into leis. They're also popular on the second-hand market: hermit crabs are quite fond of a dove shell.

Scallops

Scallops are bivalves found all over the world, but never in fresh water. By bivalves, we mean they have two valves—two hinged sides of the shell, with one side often deeper than the other. (That's the side they sit on.) Scallops can live up to twenty years, and some are male and female while other varieties are spontaneous hermaphrodites. While they might not be so good-looking, they're very good AT looking. Scallops have up to a hundred tiny eyes, each with a double-layered retina—one layer responding to light and the other responding to sudden darkness. Scallops need all these eyes to avoid predators (like starfish) because they move around, unlike their more stuck relatives, oysters and mussels. In fact, scallops can move at some speed when they need to.

Clusterwinks

They get their adorable name from grouping together like families in crevices, and clusterwinks aren't your average sea snail. They live on the rocky coastline from central Queensland, down the Australian east coast to South Australia, and they feed on microalgae. Like human families, they brood their young, but by storing them in a pouch behind their heads and releasing them as swimming larvae. Oh, and did we mention that they freaking glow? Bioluminescence, or glowing, is common in things like squids, but very, very rare in snails. But when knocked, clusterwinks emit a green flash that's produced by two patches of cells underneath their shell, which lights the whole thing up.

Violet Sea Snails

Violet sea snails get their name (somewhat unimaginatively) from their purple, or violet, shells. But while they look pretty to us, they're deadly to jellyfish and the Portuguese man o' war. See, violet sea snails drift along the surface of the ocean on 'bubble rafts', gobbling up their prey. By bubble rafts, we mean they collection of bubbles the snails create by trapping air within a mucusy substance called 'chitin'. This keeps them on the surface, where they find their prey. Violet sea snails are found in tropical and temperate oceans, and are often swept onto the beach by strong winds. You live by the bubble raft, you die by the bubble raft.

Nutmegs

Nutmeg snails are what we call Cancellariidae—a family of sea snails that live mainly in tropical waters. Their shells are solid and have a cool cross-ribbed pattern. For the most part, nutmeg snails eat plant matter and are so named because some species literally look like nutmeg. But if you think these cutely named snails are cuddly, stop reading now—before we introduce to you the Cooper's nutmeg.

>>

violet sea snail

fan scallop

clusterwink

dove

nutmeg

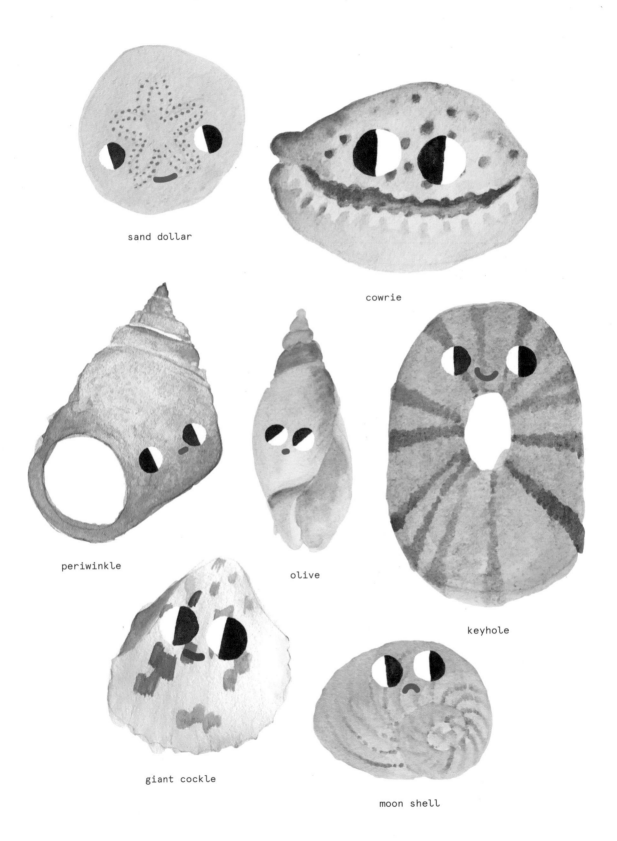

sand dollar

cowrie

periwinkle

olive

keyhole

giant cockle

moon shell

The Cooper's nutmeg feeds on electric ray blood. It uses a four-inch-long toothy snout to pierce the underside of the ray before slipping it some anaesthetic and sucking its blood for up to forty minutes, somehow without getting shocked. Ew.

Sand Dollars

You wouldn't know it from their flat shape, but sand dollars are actually sea urchins. When they're alive, they're covered in velvety spines covered in tiny hairs. These spines propel them along the ocean floor on their search for a delicious diet of larvae, algae and detritus. What we generally see of sand dollars, however, is the hard exoskeleton, or 'test'. Stripped of their velvet spines and bleached white by the sun and sea, sand dollars were thought to resemble silver coins. They also go by a heap of other, more-appetising names, like the sand cake or the sea cookie.

Cowries

They look like an unassuming, egg-shaped sea snail but for thousands of years, cowries were the money. Literally the money. In China, India and throughout Africa they were used for trade—including the slave trade. Cowries are found the world over, trolling the rocky ocean surface for food. When found they were traded; used for decorative jewellery, as a fertility symbol and in gambling games; and trafficked inland far from their rocky ocean home. The shells themselves are almost uniformly glossy and ceramic, and they have an often-toothy slit on the underside.

Periwinkles

There are about 180 species of periwinkles—or if we're being formal, the family Littorinidae. They're found worldwide and of all the sea snails, these look the most like, well, snails. They're thick, small and oval-shaped, with a sharp point. The grazing intertidal gastropods that live inside the shells feed mainly on algae, but they're also partial to animal matter, like barnacle larvae. Oh, and did we mention that they're delicious? Based on ancient middens found in Scotland, we've been eating periwinkles since 7500 BCE, and they're still sold in coastal regions of the UK and Europe, boiled and in paper bags with a handy pin attached to dig out the periwinkle-y goodness.

Cockle Shells

Another bivalve related to scallops, cockles live buried in sediment rather than roaming free like their larger, more affluent cousin. In most cases, cockle shells are ridged and heart-shaped when viewed from the end. They are found on sandy, sheltered beaches the world over and eat plankton by siphoning it between their valves. But they're best known as a snack. In the UK, they are sold boiled with malt vinegar and white pepper. In South-East Asia they might be found in a laksa. Cockles are also peppered throughout popular culture, whether they're in Mary Mary's garden or warmed in our hearts.

Keyhole Limpets

'Keyhole limpets', or 'keyhole shells', is a much better name than Fissurellidae, which is the family name. While they're sometimes called just 'limpets', they're actually pretty different to the non-keyhole variety. And not just because of the hole in the centre of their shells, after which they are named. Keyhole limpets cling to rocks with their strong suction-y feet, where they extract algae and detritus from the water. The keyhole helps water and waste product escape, to make room for more water and its sweet, life-giving algae.

Moon Shells

Rounded and glossy and often intricately patterned, moon shells are nice to look at. But underneath the shell lurks the cold heart of a killer. Using their wide foot, moon snails bore through the sand, searching for victims—mainly bivalves but also other gastropods and even other moon snails. When they find them, they drill a hole in their shell with their tongue and the help of acid secretion. And when they get in there, they use their proboscis to sup on the flesh of their prey. Pretty name, shiny shell, vicious killer.

Olives

Prized for their glossy, patterned, cylindrical shells, olive snails are carnivorous sand-burrowers. In fact, they're some of the fastest burrowers around. Some varieties can even swim a little. Living mainly in tropical waters, they have been found as far south in Australia as New South Wales. And it's not just their shells that made olive snails useful. Early Mediterranean people like the Phoenicans extracted purple dye from olive snails and their cousins, the Muricidae. This purple dye was known as Tyrian purple, imperial purple or royal purple. ///

beach trash

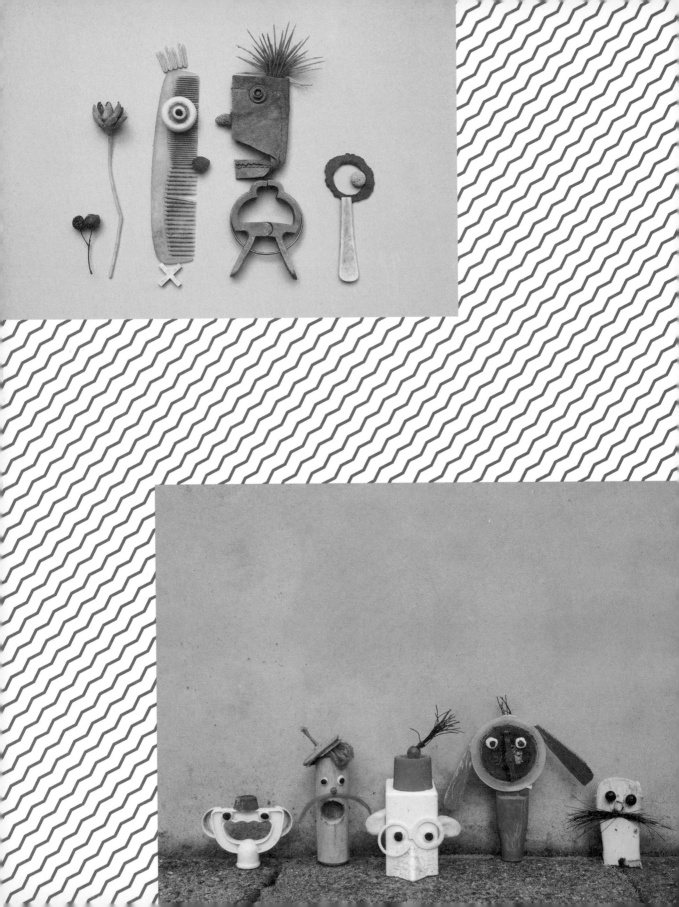

FEW people transform trash into treasure quite like Düsseldorf artist Sabine Timm. "I've been addicted to hunting treasure since my childhood," she tells me. "I remember being on vacation when I was seven and collecting shards of china from these mudflats. I still have that box and I could draw every single piece from memory. Ten years ago, when my son was seven, I took him exploring to find his own beachside treasure. No china this time, but we found shards of bleached plastic, chipped forks, flip-flop sandals and bottle caps. Everything you need for a new creation."

The fruits of this and other expeditions have become the fodder for her long-running beach trash series—or Beach Beauties, as she calls them. With a wry sense of humour and a cartoonish sensibility, Timm moulds these everyday tidbits of garbage into families of cheeky and adorable characters. Little Punk is a cracked grey cassette, with a nose made from a button, mouth a plastic ice-cream spoon and a Mohawk fashioned from a half-toothless comb. The lovely couple Boston Boy and Majorcan Girl are made from wire loops, snapped pegs, wads of old fabric and what appears to be a pink plastic battleship figurine. The range and inventiveness of her work is something to behold.

"I love the moment when I first pour my treasures out and start to organise them," she says. "My brain instantly starts creating—this looks like a nose, that's a funny mouth, what a perfect hairdo and so on. I never know what's going to come out of my playing. Often I add leaves and flowers I've found in the garden and in less than an hour a big family of new characters is born."

While much of her collection comes from the riverbanks near her home, her favourite place to go hunting is on the shores of the Mediterranean. "I go there two times a year and take these wonderful walks with our dog, Lucy. She is a very good assistant but only has eyes for driftwood. I think I am a constant hunter, though, so whenever I take a walk, I find interesting things on the ground."

Her favourite discoveries are the broken plastic toys that litter the beaches. "That's always a little feast for me! It always makes me feel like an archaeologist. These sandblasted, broken things are telling stories about the kids who played with them and the happy days they once had. It always makes me a bit sad to think of them lying in the sand, abandoned and forgotten."

Sabine sells photos of her work, but not the creatures themselves. "Some of them became beloved studio companions, and from time to time they play a role in my scenes," she explains. "The other creatures are part of the never-ending process of construction and deconstruction. I couldn't possibly let them go."

///

One lady's trash is another lady's treasure.

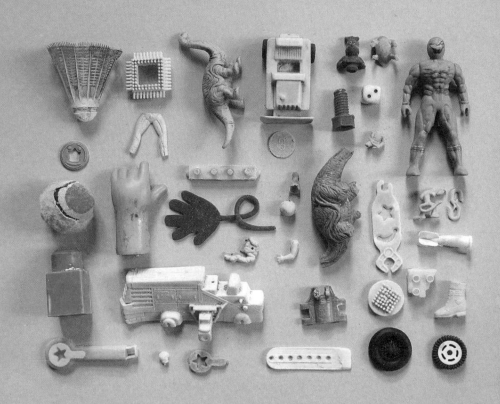

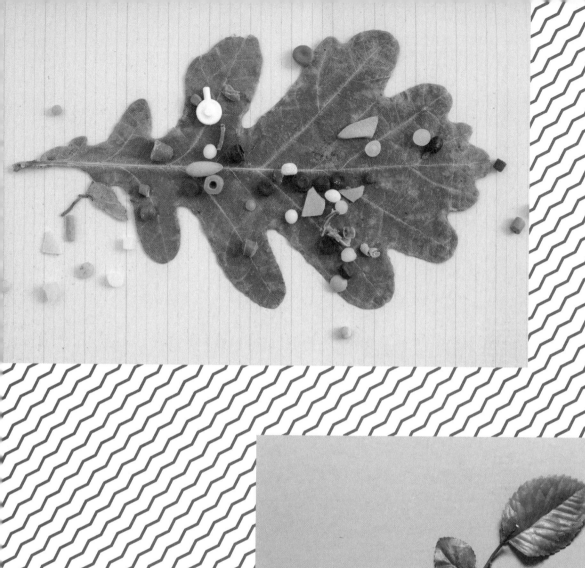

foster mums

ON THE BLOG *FOSTER MOMS*, KELLY AND JENNA TELL THE STORY OF THEIR BEAUTIFUL, IMPROVISED FAMILY IN REAL TIME. HERE THEY SHARE THE EUPHORIA, ANXIETY AND BOUNDLESS LOVE THAT COMES FROM BECOMING A FAMILY FOR THOSE WHO DON'T HAVE ONE.

In the shadow of Christmas 2014, Boston-based emergency foster parents Kelly (Therapist Mum) and Jenna (Artist Mum) were asked to take in a six-week-old African-American baby (Tiny), just for the weekend. Two weeks later, his two-and-a-half year old brother (Mr T, for toddler) came to stay. Now, three years on, they're officially a family, and their journey is only just beginning.

What first inspired you to start fostering?

Kelly: We'd known from when we first got together that we were going to be parents one day, but we always thought that we'd probably have birth kids. We weren't quite ready to make that step yet, but we were committed to the social justice element of fostering, and it seemed like a natural fit. We were both working with kids who had been involved in foster care at the time, so we had a real awareness of the need for homes for these children, especially in a temporary capacity.

Jenna: We always knew that fostering was going to be an important part of our family and that there'd be a rotating door of kids in and out of our home, because we felt like we were really well suited to provide that space for them. But we definitely weren't ready for the way it eventually happened.

Why did you choose emergency foster care?

J: Now that we're so far down the road of adoption, I can look back and say that, honestly, we had no idea what we were getting ourselves into. The way the emergency placement system works here in the States is that if a kid is pulled out of school for an investigation, or because someone has reported problems at home, and there's nowhere for that child to go overnight, then they send that kid to a home like ours in order to give themselves time to find a more permanent solution. We felt like we were shoo-ins because of our professional backgrounds, but the welcoming of pain and chaos into your home is really different in practice than you would anticipate or could even imagine.

K: I keep thinking about the first couple of kids we had. They were only supposed to be with us for twenty-four hours, but the next day would keep coming and there'd be no one to take them. I'd drop them off at school and they'd say, "Are you going to pick me up?" and I'd have to say, "I don't know. Maybe?" And that happened over and over. I knew what it was like to do long-term work with kids from these sorts of backgrounds, but when you're the one who's up at eleven at night when everyone's mad or hungry or crying,

it's a very different beast. We had this one little guy who would get in the shower fully dressed and wash his clothes, like you would do if you were homeless. How do you go back to bed after knowing that's what your home is? The whole experience was really one of professional arrogance giving way to great humility.

How did Tiny and Mr T first come into your life?

K: We'd initially said no to babies because we didn't have childcare, we both worked and we had no idea how we might look after one. But then one day we were offered this adorable six-week-old baby and in my arrogance I was just like, "What's so hard about a six-week-old baby?" After Tiny had been with us for two weeks, they called us again to say that his older brother, who was two-and-a-half, needed a placement because his current foster home couldn't deal with him. Then two weeks after that they called us to say their goal was now changing to adoption. So in less than thirty days we went from zero to two kids, with the option of forever. But it was the holiday season, so the schedule was slower; there was family around and optimism in the air. It felt like the perfect time to be building a family!

J: It was the hardest time of my life. For the first year, neither of them slept beyond forty-five minutes at

>>

We spent a lot of time with their mum during the trial for her parental rights to be terminated ... It was this very sad period of time where she was slowly coming to grips with the idea that her kids would no longer be hers, and we were coming to grips with the fact that our joy was going to be birthed from her sorrow.

a time. We were up ten or eleven times a night. It was this period of incredible, brutal adjustment for us, and at the same time we were trying to build stability and rhythm for these two fragile, tiny humans.

K: Oh, yeah. As the winter lagged on, with all the snow and the change and being trapped indoors with these two very young, very high-needs kids, it became incredibly difficult.

What was their background before they came to live with you?

K: We live in a relatively large city and there's just a huge amount of economic and environmental disparity out there. Tiny's mum grew up in an incredibly traumatic environment, so she parented in the same way she'd been parented. By the time Tiny arrived on the scene, she was twenty-six and already had three children. There was a lot of poverty and homelessness, as well as frequent moves and questionable adults coming in and out of their lives. The kids all had pretty substantial physical health concerns, as well as things like bed bugs and rodent bites.

J: The other kids had been placed in foster care before Tiny was born, so they wanted to see how she'd do with just one baby. But it became clear pretty quickly that the same concerns were happening, and that's when Tiny moved in with us.

How have your experiences of the foster system been?

K: I think the foster-care system at its core is burdened by its bureaucracy. It feels at once terribly confusing and totally predictable. But what you need to remember is that the standard of parenting for child-welfare involvement is not just a question of "good parenting"—it's parenting that is actually harmful. I think this catches a lot of foster parents off guard. You're thinking, I would never let my kids eat sugar before dinner! But harmful parenting is actually traumatising and physically impactful.

It just gets difficult when you have a different expectation from what the system does. I'll call and leave a message, but I know that my concern is not going to be within the top thirty crises that our case workers will have to deal with that day. I might need Tiny's insurance information for a doctor's appointment, but I won't get a call back because no one has run away, and no one's missing and no one's in hospital. You just need to keep on reminding yourself that you exist within a system of crisis. If you're gonna be here for the long haul, you need to be really patient. Fifty per cent of foster parents in the United States drop out before their one-year anniversary.

Has being a same-sex couple affected your experience of the foster system?

K: We definitely get a range of responses from social workers and other families as to whether it's okay for these children to be living with two women. Who's the dad? Who takes out the trash? What about these poor boys and their gender roles?

J: Who's going to teach them to pee standing up?

K: Which is totally legitimate. We did have to outsource that. When you're part of the foster system, a lot of people have opinions about your sexuality in a way that impacts your family life. "You're really homophobic and you're also in charge of my family? Awesome!" When we first started going to foster training sessions, we were just these two lesbians sitting in a big circle of church folk. You could see them looking at Jenna and going, "I think

she was in the military." No, you just mean lesbian. It's fine.

Did questions of race ever come into your conversations about adopting Tiny and Mr T?

K: It was actually one of the most significant questions I had to ask myself: what business do two white women have raising two black boys? We talked a lot to one of my cousins, who was adopted from Colombia and looks very Afro-Caribbean, about what it was like for her to grow up in a white family in the suburbs, and how that's shaped her identity.

J: But what happens when your heart is very committed is that you tend to let it make decisions that you then really fucking hope you can live out. Almost every single decision we make about our kids' lives—from childcare to preschool to school to where we live to what playgrounds we go to—is influenced by our desire for our children to have, at least sometimes, a majority experience. To be able to have some shared identity and see themselves in others.

K: People have a lot of thoughts about our family, and it comes up in public all the time. Just the other day I was in a waiting room with the two boys and an older gentleman looked at Mr T, who's lighter-skinned, and said, "Well, he's yours ..." and then he turned to Tiny and said, "But he's not yours." He was explicitly saying the implicit assumption that everyone else makes. We always knew this was going to be an ongoing part of our parenting, so how well we answer that is going to be a huge part of their growing-up experience. >>

One of the most significant questions I had to ask myself was, "What business do two white women have raising two black boys?"

How did you make the transition towards permanency?

J: As each day, each week, would turn into a month and then another month, it became clear that if adoption was the path, they were going to stay with us. They had a mum who wanted them very much as well, but she just couldn't take care of them. We spent a lot of time with her during the trial for her parental rights to be terminated. It was this very moving, very sad period of time where she was slowly coming to grips with the idea that her kids would no longer be hers, and we were coming to grips with the fact that our joy was going to be birthed from her sorrow. So adopting our boys was never going to feel out-and-out celebratory. But we have an open adoption, so they'll always know who she is and will have the option of getting to know her.

K: Going through that year-and-a-half court process was a staccato rhythm of terror and anxiety. We'd have a court date but then the judge would be too busy to see us, and then we'd have to wait for another three and a half months. There were probably a good six months where I was convinced we were going to lose because our case was so weak, or the workers were so disorganised. I remember vividly going home after court and every time just telling myself, This will probably be the last night I put my children to bed. I remember talking to friends and thinking, None of you get it. They'd say, "Oh, I remember being so anxious when I was waiting for my due date," and I'd be like, "Yeah, it's kinda different." It's really

specific—you're all the way in and then you just have to wait with bated breath. A year and a half is a long time to live in that kind of limbo.

J: I think we both aged about six years.

K: I wasn't prepared for how much this uncertainty shapes your parenting. Here are these little people, whom you are so physically connected to, and you're just so aware of how temporary your love might be. It shapes parenting in a way that's not helpful unless you do it well, and I don't think I did it well for a while there.

How did Tiny and Mr T's older brother and sister come into your life—and leave it?

K: I blame the gym. I was at the gym when they first called about Tiny, and I was at the gym when they called this time to say they didn't have a bed for their older siblings and could they come stay with us for the weekend. And I called Jenna, and Jenna was not super excited. But I was like, "We can do this!"

J: And that's how we ended up with four kids for almost three months.

K: Their brother moved out at the end of last summer and their sister has been with us ever since. Before they moved in they didn't really have the identity of being siblings because they'd been in foster care for four years and hadn't ever lived together, all four of them, as a family. Now that we've been together for a year, our sense of family and their sister's sense of siblings is really different. She's in the process of moving to her adopted

forever home, which is great, but also painful and scathing and all of that.

J: Of course we asked ourselves the question of whether we could make it work, but all the kids have really significant needs and three or four is just more than we could handle. There's an expectation in fostering that kids always do better together, but we had to be brutally honest with ourselves about our capacities and what it would mean to give these kids the best life possible.

K: Even from an attachment perspective, we could see that the numbers weren't working: all four kids wanted to be picked up or sit on my lap all the time, so there was a constant sense of who was getting picked and who wasn't. When the older brother moved to his new family, we spent a long time trying to see if three was going to be sustainable. We swung back and forth a lot on that. But all these kids have substantial learning and executive function challenges, so even from a financial standpoint there was this question of, can we afford to provide the care these kids need?

J: We just had to have faith that the time Tiny and Mr T's sister spent in our family and the time she spent at school—this was her first time in the same school for an entire year—was going to set her up for whatever was going to happen next. If we were going to continue to believe that there was justice in this process, then the right family would surface and we would have made the right choice.

I'm so aware that we're our boys' plan-B, even if they're our plan-A. They should have been able to be raised by family who look like them and gave birth to them and can keep them safe, but that couldn't happen, so here we are.

Will the kids continue to have
sibling contact with each other?

K: Absolutely. We've been very clear
on this since last summer—they
have become a family. The only
way to honourably manage this is
for them to continue to be siblings
who just live in different houses.
The best model we have is with their
brother's new dad. We FaceTime
with him once a month, and we text
and send pictures of the kids to each
other so we can see what's going on
in one another's lives. That's been
our framework for what we want to
happen with Tiny and Mr T's sister,
and the case workers have been
great in trying to find a family that
will be open to sibling contact, as
well as being open to a family with
two mums. But merely having those
demands has probably meant it's
taken longer to find her the right
home. Not all parents want kids who
have attachment to other parents, or
want to be in an extended family with
people they don't know.

Have the relationships you've formed
with your kids been different to what
you thought they were going to be?

K: What's surprised me is how deeply
I see myself in them, and I worry they
won't be able to do the same with
me. My nieces and nephews—I can
tie their behaviours or appearance
to, say, my brother-in-law or their
grandmother. There's a sense of
knowing or connection that my kids
just don't have. I find myself having
these moments almost every day
where I'm almost mourning for that
lack. I'm so aware that we're our boys'
plan-B, even if they're our plan-A.
They should have been able to be
raised by family who look like them
and gave birth to them and can keep
them safe, but that couldn't happen,
so here we are. That's really shaped
my parenting: this sense of being able
to honour that responsibility.

J: When Tiny and Mr T first arrived, I
was working twelve hours a day, so my
relationship with the kids was mostly
based around dinner and putting
them to bed. I always felt this sense of
loss about not having more time with
them, but career was really important
to me back then. And now I'm with
them all day, every day. I feel like less
of a provider and more of a playmate. I
have always watched them in wonder,
but now I feel like I'm falling in love
with the people they are in this world.
Like Tiny: when we first got him, he
was this little chocolate gumdrop who
wouldn't respond when you talked
to him, and now he's this vibrant
two-and-a-half year old. He's such
a crazy normal toddler in so many
ways, just figuring out who he is in the
world, and I feel so lucky to have this
period where it's just me and them.

K: Our kids have a lot of attachment
issues, so I think another big piece for
us is being continually surprised that
that's still a thing. Today they were
with their favourite family friend,
who's like a grandmother to them,
and Mr T was crying hysterically
when he had to leave. There's always
this subtext of trauma and loss that
colours what we see. That's been a
real eye-opener for me: that you fill
in the gaps with trauma. Sometimes
what you're seeing might be normal,
sometimes it might not, but trauma is
always the default response.

How has writing about your
experience helped you to process all
the craziness of the past three years?

K: Initially we thought that the blog
could be a way of making families
like ours more visible and finding a
community of people going through
similar things. But now I see it more
as the baby book of our family: the
story of how we became who we are. I
hope one day I can give it to our kids
as a gift of this time, an explanation
of all the things we felt as we made
our family, and how honoured I feel
to have taken on this responsibility.
I'm parenting for both of us: for their
mum, in her stead, and for me, in
my own. There's so much day-to-day
bullshit that can get in the way; it's
nice to have something that reminds
you of what matters.

J: The blog was my idea originally.
I thought it was an important way
of connecting with Kelly as we
went through all of this—creating
a thread that kept us coming back
together. There's never been a goal
or expectation around it, but for me
it's become a time capsule in a lot of
really nice ways.

K: It really makes you realise how
boringly normal we actually are. But
that mundanity is part of normalising
same-sex parenting and foster care:
we deal with the same boring stuff that
everyone else deals with. Kids deserve
to have boring, normal families doing
boring, normal family stuff. That's
when you know it's working.

How has becoming a parent changed
your own relationship?

K: It has really forced us to figure out
how to screen for what matters. The
bottom-line question for both of us
all the time is, who do we want to be
for these two young boys? What does
our home need to be to give them the
best chance in this world? It's pushed
us into a more grown-up version of
love that's just really different than
before. Co-parenting is one of the
most intimate and challenging and
rewarding things you can do with
somebody else. We perhaps thought
we were a lot more aligned as parents
than we actually ended up being. And
a lot of those differences are small,
but it requires constant negotiation.

J: It's been a really humbling
experience. You don't just wake up
being a more grown-up version of
yourself. You actually have to change
habits that have been ingrained from
day one. It brings up a lot for me
personally, but it also reaffirms over
and over that Kelly's my person. Even
though I knew when I met her that I
wanted to have a family with her, now
that we have one I'm even more certain
that she's the one I want to do it with.
///

tarts

APPLE + PISTACHIO PRALINE POP TART

For the dough:
- 2 cups plain flour
- 1 tbsp sugar
- 1 tsp salt
- 1 cup unsalted butter, cut into cubes
- 1 egg
- 2 tbsp milk
- 1 egg, lightly beaten for brushing pastry

For the apple filling:
- 2 medium apples
- 1/3 cup dark brown sugar, packed
- 1 1/2 tsp lemon juice
- 1/2 tsp ground cinnamon
- 1/2 tsp salt

For the icing:
- 3/4 cup icing sugar
- 2 tbsp reserved apple-cinnamon filling juices
- 2 tsp lemon juice
- 2 tsp milk, plus more as needed

For the praline (optional):
- 1/2 cup pistachios
- 1 1/2 cups caster sugar

1. To make the dough, place flour, sugar and salt into a food processor and pulse until combined.

2. Add butter and pulse until the mixture turns into pea-sized clumps.

3. Pour the mixture into a bowl.

4. Whisk the egg and milk together and then add them to the dough, mixing just until everything is well combined.

5. Tip onto a well-floured surface and knead until you have a smooth dough.

6. Divide dough in half and shape each half into a rough rectangle. Wrap both in plastic wrap, and refrigerate for 30 minutes.

7. For the apple filling, peel and core the apples, and cut them first into 5mm-thick slices and then into thirds.

8. Combine all filling ingredients in a frying pan over medium heat.

9. Cook, stirring constantly, until sugar has dissolved and the apple juices begin to release—about 5 minutes.

10. Continue cooking until apples just begin to soften— about 3 minutes more. Remove from heat.

11. Pop a strainer over a bowl and pour apples and juices into the strainer. Set aside to cool.

12. For the praline, add sugar to a small pan and cook to a medium-coloured caramel. Shake the pan regularly to cook evenly. Do not stir.

13. Once caramel has turned desired colour, remove from heat and pour onto a lined tray.

14. Sprinkle pistachios over caramel and allow to cool.

15. Once cooled, add the caramel to a food processor and whiz until you've got a coarse sprinkling consistency. Set aside.

16. Preheat oven to 190°C / 375°F / Gas Mark 5.

17. Line another baking tray with baking paper.

18. Lightly dust your bench with flour and roll the first dough out into a rough 30cm x 25cm rectangle. Regularly turn the dough and re-flour the bench and rolling pin to prevent the dough from sticking.

19. Using a pizza cutter or sharp knife and a ruler, cut the dough into a 25cm x 20cm rectangle. Then cut it into 6 equal rectangles.

20. Using a spatula, place the rectangles onto the lined baking tray, leaving about 5cm of space between each.

21. Pop the baking tray in the fridge.

22. Whisk egg and water in a small bowl, and set aside.

23. Roll out the second dough to the same dimensions as the first. Trim and cut into 6 rectangles.

24. Using a fork, prick the dough all over.

25. Pop 2 tablespoons of the cooled apple juices into a medium bowl and set it aside for the glaze. Set the remaining juices aside, too.

26. Remove the baking tray from the fridge and brush a thin coating of egg wash over each dough rectangle.

27. Spoon about 1 heaped tablespoon of the apple filling onto each rectangle and spread it into an even layer, leaving a 2cm border.

28. Top each rectangle with 1 1/2 teaspoons of the remaining apple juices.

29. Place the pricked rectangles on top of the apple-covered rectangles.

30. Press on the edges and push down gently on the filling to slightly flatten it. Using a fork dipped in flour, crimp the edges of the tarts.

31. Bake until golden brown— about 23-25 minutes.

32. Transfer to a wire rack and allow to cool completely.

33. While the pop tarts are cooling, make the icing.

34. Place all ingredients into a small bowl and whisk until evenly combined.

35. Spoon a thin layer of icing on top of the cooled pop tarts.

36. Allow icing to harden a little and then sprinkle with praline if using.

37. Place the pop tarts onto a baking tray and let them harden, uncovered, for about 2 hours.

///

CHOCOLATE PNB POP TART

For the dough:
- 2 cups plain flour
- 2 tbsp cocoa
- 1 tbsp sugar
- 1 tsp salt
- 1 cup unsalted butter, cut into cubes
- 1 egg
- 2 tbsp milk
- 1 egg, lightly beaten for brushing pastry

For the peanut butter filling:
- 1/2 cup smooth peanut butter
- 1 tbsp butter, softened
- 1 tbsp icing sugar
- 1 tsp vanilla extract

For the icing:
- 1 cup icing sugar
- 1 tbsp vanilla extract
- 1 tbsp cocoa
- 3 tbsp water
- 1/4 cup milk chocolate, melted

For the garnish:
- 1/4 cup crushed honeycomb

1. To make the dough, place flour, cocoa, sugar and salt into a food processor and pulse until combined.

2. Add butter and pulse until the mixture turns into pea-sized clumps.

3. Pour the mixture into a bowl.

4. Whisk the egg and milk together, and then add them to the dough, mixing just until everything is well combined.

5. Tip onto a well-floured surface and knead until you have a smooth dough.

6. Divide dough in half and shape each half into a rough rectangle. Wrap both in plastic wrap, and refrigerate for 30 minutes.

7. For the peanut butter fudge filling, beat together the peanut butter, butter, powdered sugar and vanilla in a mixing bowl until smooth and creamy. Set aside.

8. Preheat oven to 190°C / 375°F / Gas Mark 5.

9. Line a baking tray with baking paper.

10. Lightly dust your bench with flour and roll the first dough out into a rough 30cm x 25cm rectangle. Regularly turn the dough and re-flour the bench and rolling pin to prevent the dough from sticking.

11. Using a pizza cutter or sharp knife and a ruler, cut the dough into a 25cm x 20cm rectangle. Then cut it into 6 equal rectangles.

12. Using a spatula, place the rectangles onto the lined baking tray, leaving about 5cm of space between each.

13. Pop the baking tray in the fridge.

14. Whisk egg and water in a small bowl, and set aside.

15. Roll out the second dough to the same dimensions as the first. Trim it and cut into 6 rectangles.

16. Using a fork, prick the dough all over.

17. Remove the baking tray from the fridge and brush a thin coating of egg wash over each dough rectangle.

19. Spoon about 1 heaped tablespoon of the peanut butter filling onto each rectangle and spread it into an even layer, leaving a 2cm border.

20. Place the pricked rectangles on top of the peanut butter-covered rectangles.

21. Press on the edges and push down gently on the filling to slightly flatten it. Using a fork dipped in flour, crimp the edges of the tarts.

22. Bake until golden brown— about 23-25 minutes.

23. Transfer to a wire rack and allow to cool completely.

24. While the pop tarts are cooling, make the icing.

25. Mix icing sugar, vanilla, cocoa and 3 tablespoons of water for about 7-10 minutes on medium speed in an electric mixer, until peaks begin to form.

28. Stir in the melted chocolate. If icing seems too thick, thin it by adding more water.

29. Spoon a thin layer of icing on top of the cooled pop tarts.

30. Allow icing to harden a little and then sprinkle with honeycomb.

31. Place the pop tarts onto a baking tray and let them harden, uncovered, for about 2 hours.

///

RASPBERRY +
PEACH POP TART

For the dough:
- 2 cups plain flour
- 2 tbsp cocoa
- 1 tbsp sugar
- 1 tsp salt
- 1 cup unsalted butter,
  cut into cubes
- 1 egg
- 2 tbsp milk
- 1 egg, lightly beaten for
  brushing pastry

For the fruit filling:
- 2 tbsp white sugar
- 2 tsp cornflour
- 1/2 tsp nutmeg, grated
- 1/4 tsp ground cinnamon
- pinch of salt
- 1 cup raspberries
- 1 small peach, peeled,
  pitted and diced

For the icing:
- 1/2 cup icing sugar
- 115g / 4oz cream cheese,
  at room temperature
- 1 tsp vanilla extract
- 2-3 tbsp milk, at room
  temperature
- 2-3 tsp raspberry juices,
  from filling

For the garnish:
- 1/4 cup shredded coconut

1. To make the dough, place flour, sugar and salt into a food processor and pulse until combined.

2. Add butter and pulse until the mixture turns into pea-sized clumps.

3. Pour mixture into a bowl.

4. Whisk the egg and milk together, and then add them to the dough, mixing just until everything is well combined.

5. Tip onto a well-floured surface and knead until you have a smooth dough.

6. Divide dough in half and shape each half into a rough rectangle. Wrap both in plastic wrap, and refrigerate for 30 minutes.

7. For the filling, in a small saucepan, whisk together sugar, cornflour, nutmeg, cinnamon and salt.

8. Stir in raspberries and peach and cook over medium heat until the fruit has broken down and the mixture has thickened—about 6-8 minutes.

9. Spoon out a couple of tablespoons of the juices and reserve for the icing. Leave to cool completely.

10. Preheat oven to 190°C / 375°F / Gas Mark 5.

11. Line a baking tray with baking paper.

12. Lightly dust your bench with flour and roll the first dough rectangle out into a rough 30cm x 25cm rectangle. Regularly turn the dough and re-flour the bench and rolling pin often to prevent the dough from sticking.

13. Using a pizza cutter or sharp knife and a ruler, cut the dough into a 25cm x 20cm rectangle. Then cut it into 6 equal rectangles.

14. Using a spatula, place the rectangles onto the lined baking tray, leaving about 5cm of space between each.

15. Pop the baking tray in the fridge.

16. Whisk egg and water in a small bowl, and set aside.

17. Roll out the second dough rectangle to the same dimensions as the first. Trim it and cut into 6 rectangles.

18. Using a fork, prick the dough all over.

19. Remove the baking tray from the fridge and brush a thin coating of egg wash over each dough rectangle.

20. Spoon about 1 heaped tablespoon of the fruit filling onto each rectangle and spread it into an even layer, leaving a 2cm border.

21. Place the pricked rectangles on top of the fruit-covered rectangles.

22. Press on the edges and push down gently on the filling to slightly flatten it. Using a fork dipped in flour, crimp the edges of the tarts.

23. Bake until golden brown— about 23-25 minutes.

24. Transfer to a wire rack and allow to cool completely.

25. While the pop tarts are cooling, make the icing.

26. Whisk together icing sugar, cream cheese and vanilla in a small bowl.

28. Spoon a thin layer of icing on top of the cooled pop tarts.

29. Allow icing to harden a little and then sprinkle with coconut.

30. Place the pop tarts onto a baking tray and let them harden, uncovered, for about 2 hours.

///

World first beehive that harvests honey straight from a tap !

sweet as

honey

Like air and water, honey has existed on Earth since forever. Which is something to stop and think about next time you're spreading some over your toast in the morning. What you're about to enjoy isn't just another tasty spread; it's an ancient source of nutrition, literally unchanged for millennia.

The oldest bee fossils date back over one hundred million years, and humans have been harvesting honey from the moment they climbed down from the trees. Actually, before then, when we were still swinging around the branches. As far as backstories go, it's a pretty sweet one.

Honey's history is global, too. Traced from cave paintings in Spain (which show two hunters attacking a nest of bees) to clay vessels in Georgia (unearthed from an age-old tomb) to the records of ancient Greece, where a law was written that said: "He who sets up hives of bees must put them 300 feet away from those already installed by another."

In Australia, where native species already existed, the early settlers introduced honey bees. Missing the comforts of home back in England, they brought some bees with them aboard the ship *Isabella* in 1822. The new critters adapted so well that different species were later introduced from other parts of Europe and North America, laying the foundations for the local honey industry today. It's almost enough to forgive the colonists for bringing pests like lantana and foxes with them too.

CULTURAL SIGNIFICANCE

Today, the primary uses for honey are basically unchanged from centuries past. Most people eat it, or add it as a sweetener, while others think of it as more of a medicine. Lesser known is the fact that honey has always carried some religious significance.

For Buddhists in India and Bangladesh, honey plays an important role in the festival Madhu Purnima, which celebrates the day Buddha bolted into the wilderness before making peace between his disciples. Legend has it that, while Buddha was hanging out, a thoughtful little monkey brought him some honey to mung on. So on Madhu Purnima each year, Buddhists remember this random act of kindness by giving jars of honey to local monks.

In the classic Greek myths, the food of Zeus and his posse was a honey-like substance known as 'ambrosia'. Delivered by doves, it was said to make the gods immortal, which is pretty cool as far as health benefits go.

The Hebrew Bible makes references to honey all over the place. From the lesser-known proverb that says, "Pleasant words are as a honeycomb, sweet to the soul, and health to the bones," to the Book of Exodus, which famously describes the Promised Land as "flowing with milk and honey". Interestingly, pure honey is considered kosher, even though it's made by a non-kosher creature— the only foodstuff the rules were rewritten for. Honey's also the star of the Jewish New Year get-together, Rosh Hashanah, where the traditional meal includes apple slices dipped in honey in the hopes of delivering a sweet new year.

USES

You can apply honey to burns, drink it as a tonic and even turn it into booze, yet the primary use of honey is still just as a yummy food. From our early memories of scoffing honey joys at birthday parties and binging on old-school honey chicken—that beloved dish at Chinese restaurants around Australia—to pretty much every baked good and sweet treat worthy of being on a dessert menu, honey is often the hero ingredient. It's the great all-rounder: if you get tired of the delicious breads, cookies and cakes made with honey, you can get your fix from the various teas, sauces, dressings, drinks and spreads that have it in them, too.

Medicinally, we're all familiar with honey being used as a natural cough syrup, but it turns out the science might not back that up. That's not to say honey doesn't deserve a place in your medicine cabinet, because it's been proven to have surprising wound-healing properties. Thanks to it containing certain bioactive components, applying honey externally can have amazing results on burns and other injuries.

While eating too much isn't good for you, when it's used as a natural wound dressing honey's been proven to have the same healing properties as a number of man-made drugs, with the added benefit of having them all working together at once to speed up the healing process. Just the physical properties of honey alone are enough to help, according to researchers, because it's acidic, which helps create conditions where tissue can start repairing itself. And because of its high sugar content, which draws water out of the wound, it can stop any nasty bacteria from growing.

But not all honey's the same. Some varieties are up to 100 times more potent! Manuka's generally considered the best medicinal honey, due to the concentration of an antibacterial component called methylglyoxal. In one clinical trial, where manuka honey was applied to chronic pressure ulcers, eighteen out of twenty patients were completely healed after four weeks.

And while it's still early days, there's also a growing scientific movement around using honey to treat allergies that are triggered by pollen—the theory being that small, daily doses of honey harvested from your local area (and therefore produced from local pollen) can help build up an immunity over time.

Then there's that other wonder drug: alcohol. Honey's the main ingredient in mead, commonly known as 'honey wine'. Knocked back during ancient happy hours across Europe, Africa and Asia, mead is a simple booze made by fermenting honey and water. With its easy-drinking flavour and alcohol levels that range anywhere from eight to twenty per cent, it's a nice way to get your, ahem, buzz on.

Even if getting pickled isn't your thing, you can use honey to preserve nearly anything. Thanks primarily to the might of sugar, not only can honey sit on your shelf for ages, but there are also records of ancient artifacts (including the remains of various emperors and kings) immersed in honey that have been maintained for centuries. Whether it's a body or a beetroot, the way it works is that the high sugar content squeezes the water content out of any yeast or bacteria cells, which would normally contaminate any food (or corpses).

HOW IT'S MADE

By now it's no secret that bees are rad. This sweet, magical golden liquid that we use to treat and heal ourselves with—it's what they spew up after eating a gutful of nectar. Think about how different that is from humans who eat too much of something.

First, the honey bee cruises around looking for sugar-rich nectar—found in flowers—which it initially uses like an energy drink so it can keep foraging for more nectar. Eventually returning to the hive, the bees eat and regurgitate the nectar repeatedly until it's partially digested. This part of the process takes around twenty minutes, or until the drone bee who's handling quality control deems the product to be storage-quality. That's when it's placed into the honeycomb cells, but they're left unsealed, because there's too much water and natural yeast present in the liquid, and that would cause the honey to ferment. So then what do the industrious little buggers do? They team up and flutter their wings to circulate air around the hive, like a bee-driven AC, and this evaporates the water, raises the sugar content, and stops the honey from fermenting and blowing up the cells. To top it all off, literally, the bees cap each cell with a perfect wax seal.

All this happens out in the wild, obviously, but with the invention of the man-made beehive in 1814 we managed to industrialise the process, too. So now there are small wooden bee hotels all over the world with removable frames inside, and once the honey's ready, a beekeeper comes around, smokes the bees out and steals the goods, leaving just enough for them to survive the winter.

>>

Legend has it that, while Buddha was hanging out, a thoughtful little monkey brought him some honey to mung on. So each year, Buddhists remember this random act of kindness by giving jars of honey to local monks.

HONEY + GINGER COUGH SYRUP

• zest of 2 lemons • 1/4 cup ginger, peeled and sliced
• 1 cup water • 1 cup honey • 1/2 cup lemon juice

In a small saucepan, add lemon zest, sliced ginger
and 1 cup of water, and stir to combine. Bring to a boil
and simmer for 5 minutes. Strain into a cup or jug and
set aside. Rinse out the saucepan and pour in honey.
Warm honey over a low heat. Do not let it boil. Add the
strained lemon ginger water and lemon juice. Stir until
it forms a thick syrup. Pour into a clean jar with
a lid. This can be refrigerated for up to 2 months.

*Directions: For children ages 1-5, use 1/2-1 teaspoon
every 2 hours. For children ages 5-12, use 1-2 teaspoons
every 2 hours. For children 12+ and adults, use 1-2
tablespoons every 4 hours. *Honey is recommended
for children OVER the age of one.*

- - -

When it's used as a natural wound dressing, honey's been proven to have the same healing properties as a number of man-made drugs—it's acidic, which helps create conditions where tissue can start repairing itself. And because of its high sugar content, which draws water out of the wound, it can stop any nasty bacteria from growing.

<<

NUTRITIONAL STUFF

There's no dodging the fact that honey is basically just sugar syrup. Except for around 15 per cent water, there's almost nothing in it except a tasty blend of fructose, glucose, maltose and sucrose. Of course, the colour, aroma and flavour all change depending on the type of flowers the bees use to produce it, but not much else. True, there's also pollen, mineral, vitamins and antioxidants, but not enough to make a huge impact on your diet. No, the only real benefit of eating honey instead of sugar is that honey takes longer to digest, providing more of a slow-burn energy.

VARIETIES

While we generally think of it as golden liquid stuck in a jar, or possibly some sort of bear-shaped vessel, honey comes in all sorts of varieties and it's subject to all sorts of industrial processing.

One of the most common natural variations is crystallised honey, which occurs when some of the glucose spontaneously turns into bigger sugar crystals. Also known as candied honey, it's easily returned to its natural liquid state just by warming it up a bit. Creamed honey, or whipped honey, is made by controlling this crystallisation process, so there are lots of tiny crystals, which makes it smooth and spreadable, with a creamy colour.

There's dried honey, which has had all the moisture extracted from it; comb honey, which is still inside the wax comb; and strained honey, which has been passed through a big sieve to remove anything foreign without losing all the good stuff. And this is where it gets interesting, because there's an enormous difference between raw honey and one that's been filtered or pasteurised.

The definition of raw honey is anything that exists the same way it would inside the beehive. It might have been extracted, settled or strained, but never heated. Treated this way, it might contain the occasional bit of wax, but at least it still holds all the antibacterial and anti-inflammatory goodness.

On the other hand, pasteurised honey has been heated to a temperature of 72 degrees Celsius or higher, mostly in order to kill off any yeast cells, so there's no chance the honey can start fermenting. Worse still, some commercial honey is watered down and forced through extremely fine filters, removing everything including the pollen, before other sugars and syrups are added to change the look and taste. Just like [insert your favourite industrial farming nightmare here], honey's way cheaper to produce this way, but the bastardised version has almost no redeeming features from a health perspective.

How can you spot the difference between honey and (p)honey, besides checking the label on the bottle, which can be misleading? It's not hard. Just fill a glass of water and add a tablespoon of the 'honey' to it. The raw stuff will clump together and settle at the bottom, while the 'phoney' will start dissolving straight away.

PLAN BEE

For something that's been around so long, it's no exaggeration to say we're only just starting to realise honey's potential. From sweet treat to powerful medicine, who knows what its future applications will include? Hopefully we can save the honey bees and take care of the planet long enough to find out.

///

HONEY + TAHINI BICCIES

- 1/2 cup sesame seeds
- 1 1/2 cups almond meal
- 1/2 tsp baking soda
- 1/4 tsp sea salt
- 1/3 cup honey
- 1/3 cup tahini
- 1 tsp vanilla extract

1. Preheat oven to 180°C / 350°F / Gas Mark 4.

2. Line 2 baking sheets with baking paper.

3. Pour sesame seeds onto a bread plate.

4. In a small bowl, whisk together almond meal, baking soda and salt.

5. In a large bowl, mix together honey, tahini and vanilla extract.

6. Add dry ingredients to wet ingredients and stir until well combined.

7. Scoop tablespoons of dough, and roll into balls.

8. Roll each ball in the sesame seeds, and then flatten into rounds.

9. Pop the rounds onto the baking sheets, approximately 5cm apart.

10. Bake for 8 minutes, until the bottoms are golden. Swap the trays from top to bottom of the oven halfway through cooking.

11. Cool biccies on a wire rack.

///

TURMERIC, BLACK PEPPER + HONEY TEA

- 1/3 cup honey
- 2 1/2 tsp ground turmeric
- squeeze of lemon
- pepper, ground

1. Mix turmeric and honey together to form a paste. This can be kept in a jar for later use.

2. For each cup of tea, pop a teaspoon of paste in a mug.

3. Top with almost-boiling water.

4. Add a squeeze of lemon and a crack of freshly ground pepper.

///

SAGE + HONEY SKILLET CORNBREAD

<u>Makes 10 to 12 serves</u>

- 1 cup cornmeal
- 1 cup plain flour
- 1 tbsp baking powder
- 1 tsp salt
- 2 tsp fresh sage leaves, chopped
- 12 whole fresh sage leaves
- 1 cup whole milk
- 1/2 cup honey
- 1 free-range egg
- 1/2 cup unsalted butter

1. Preheat oven to 200°C / 400°F / Gas Mark 6. Heat a heavy, 10-inch diameter ovenproof skillet (preferably cast-iron) in the oven for 10 minutes.

2. Whisk first 4 ingredients and 2 teaspoons of chopped fresh sage in a large bowl to blend.

3. Whisk milk, honey and egg in a medium bowl to blend.

4. Remove skillet from oven. Add 1/2 cup butter, and swirl until butter is melted. Pour all of it except 2 tablespoons into the egg mixture. Add whole sage leaves to butter in the skillet, and toss to coat. Arrange leaves over the bottom of the skillet, spacing them apart.

5. Add egg mixture to cornmeal mixture and stir until just combined. (Do not overmix, or else batter will be wet and runny.)

6. Pour batter over the sage leaves in the skillet.

7. Pop in oven and bake until browned around edges and a skewer inserted into the centre comes out clean— about 22 minutes.

8. Cool in skillet for 10 minutes before turning out onto a platter. If necessary, reposition sage leaves on top of the cornbread.

///

goat's milk, honey + oats soap !

Makes approx. 4 standard bars

- 450g / 1lb goat's milk melt-and-pour soap base
- 2 tbsp organic honey
- 3/4 cup organic oats
- silicone soap moulds (we used 4 moulds around 8cm wide x 5cm long x 3cm deep, each with a capacity of approximately 115g / 0.25lb)

1. Fill saucepan with water and bring to a boil while you prepare the other ingredients.

2. Cut the melt-and-pour soap base into cubes and place in a bowl.

3. Set the bowl on top of the saucepan and allow the cubes to melt, stirring occasionally with a skewer or chopstick to keep the mixture smooth and to break up any lumps.

4. Once fully melted, add the oats and mix through.

5. Pour the mixture into soap moulds. Use the tea towel or oven mitt so you don't burn yourself on the hot bowl.

6. Drizzle honey evenly into each soap mould, and then use the skewer or chopstick to gently mix it through.

7. Let the soap set for 1 hour or until firm.

8. Carefully remove bars from the silicone moulds by turning them upside down and pushing lightly on the back of each bar while gently peeling back the mould.

vanilla + honey lip balm !

Makes approx. 3 small pots

- 3 tsp beeswax (we used palm-free, organic beeswax pellets as they are easier to measure and melt than solid beeswax bars)
- 2 tbsp shea butter
- 2 tbsp sweet almond oil (or jojoba oil if you are allergic to almonds)
- 1 1/2 tsp raw honey
- 1/2 tsp pure vanilla extract
- small pots with lids for storing the balm (we used 30ml glass pots)

1. Fill saucepan with water and bring to a boil while you prepare the other ingredients.

2. Combine beeswax, shea butter and sweet almond oil in a bowl and place on top of saucepan. Allow the mixture to melt fully, stirring continuously with a skewer or chopstick to ensure it is smooth and free of lumps.

3. Using a tea towel or oven mitt to protect your hands, remove the mixture from the heat and add honey and vanilla extract, stirring continuously to ensure it blends well. The beeswax will start to solidify, so you'll need to work rather quickly to make sure you get a smooth blend.

4. Pour mixture into glass pots, and leave them to cool and set completely.

////

Due to the natural ingredients in these recipes, we recommend storing in a cool place away from direct sunlight and using them within 6 months.

HONEY + ROSEWATER CAKE

For the cake:
- 170g / 6oz honey
- 140g / 5oz butter
- 80g / 2.8oz brown sugar
- 1 tbsp
- 2 free-range eggs, beaten
- 200g / 7oz self-raising flour, sifted

For the icing:
- 3 tbsp honey
- 1/2 tsp baking soda
- 170g unsalted butter, room temperature
- 3/4 cup icing sugar
- 1/4 tsp fine salt
- 3/4 tsp rose water
- bee pollen, for garnish
- edible flowers, for garnish

1. Preheat oven to 180°C / 350°F / Gas Mark 3.

2. Grease and line a cake tin.

3. Add honey, butter, sugar and water to a saucepan over low heat, and stir until melted.

4. Remove from heat and mix in eggs and flour.

5. Pour into cake tin and bake for 40-45 minutes until cake is springy and shrinking away from the sides of the tin.

6. Cool in the tin for a few minutes before turning out onto a wire rack to cool further. While it does, make the icing.

8. Pop honey in a small saucepan and heat on medium until it just begins to bubble. Turn off heat, add baking soda and whisk well, making sure to get rid of any lumps. Set aside to cool.

9. In the bowl of an electric mixer, beat butter for 3-5 minutes until pale.

10. Slowly pour in the cooled honey and beat until well mixed.

11. Sift icing sugar over butter and beat on low. Scrape down the sides of the bowl when needed.

12. Add salt and rosewater, and beat on high for a further 3-5 minutes until creamy and light.

13. Once the cake has completely cooled, ice it and decorate it with bee pollen and flowers.

///

HONEY + ORANGE PEKOE TEA LOAF

For the cake:
- 1 1/2 cups sultanas
- zest and juice of 1 orange
- 1/4 cup honey
- 1 cup boiling orange pekoe tea, strong
- 2 free-range eggs, beaten
- 1 1/2 cups wholemeal flour
- 1/2 cup rolled oats
- 1 tbsp baking powder

1. Pop sultanas, orange zest, orange juice and honey into a large bowl and pour tea over the ingredients. Leave to soak for 2 hours.

2. Grease and line a loaf tin.

3. Preheat oven to 200°C / 400°F / Gas Mark 6.

4. Mix eggs into the sultana mixture.

5. In a separate bowl, mix together flour, oats and baking powder.

6. Add flour mixture to sultana mixture and stir until combined.

7. Pour mixture into the loaf tin and bake for 45-50 minutes, until golden brown. Insert a skewer in the centre; if it comes out clean, the cake is done.

8. Allow the cake to cool slightly before turning it out of the tin.

9. Leave to cool on a wire rack.

///

To bee or not to bee

A young scientist from France, Simon Klein is carrying on a tradition started by the Académie des sciences, which stretches back over 300 years to when King Louis XIV founded it. Better known for its contribution to the arts, France has constantly been at the forefront of scientific advances, too, in fields ranging from chemistry to medicine to nuclear power.

A humble homme who's already won the respect of his peers, Klein's led discoveries into the enigmatic world of bee navigation, studying their tiny brains and reporting back with some remarkable finds, including the revelation that bees use natural landmarks the same way humans use signposts. And yet, despite his own amazing research, Klein's favourite fact about bees is one that was unearthed way back in the 1940s by another European brain.

Previously, bees were thought to use a combination of smell and taste to give each other directions. But the Austrian professor Karl von Frisch discovered bees actually tell one another where to find the best flowers by shakin' their butts. "I still think that's the most surprising thing about bees," says Klein. "Inside the hive, you've got dance floors and some bees looking at other bees wiggling their arses, talking to each other with a dance."

Sadly, after bees had boogied their way through the centuries, the never-ending bee party was interrupted ten years ago when US beekeepers suddenly and mysteriously found that their hives were nearly all empty.

What started off like the opening scene of a sci-fi thriller ended up being a real phenomenon known as 'colony collapse disorder'. In case you haven't heard, that's when bees everywhere started dropping like flies due to increased parasites and pesticides, and the plants that they need to survive were either being destroyed completely or not behaving the way bees were used to, due to a changing climate.

Now maybe you're someone who doesn't like honey or thinks that losing an insect that stings people is not such a bad thing, but even so, consider this lone fact: a third of the crops humans consume in a regular diet, from basic grains used to bake bread to the beans that make your morning coffee, would fail without bees around to pollinate them. That means that without bees the Western industrial food complex would collapse—and yet there's no plan Bee to try and save them.

Absolutely critical when it comes to their role in the ecosystem, bees are much more than just honey-making machines. While some birds, bats and even a few monkeys are pollinators, bees do the heaviest lifting when it comes to helping plants reproduce all over the world. So it makes sense that we use them to help explain sex; the irony is we're all screwed if they disappear. >>

Consider this lone fact: a third of the crops humans consume in a regular diet, from basic grains used to bake bread to the beans that make your morning coffee, would fail without bees around to pollinate them.

HONEY, ROSEMARY + APPLE JAM

- 1kg / 2lb Granny Smith apples
- 4 cups cold water
- 2 big sprigs of rosemary
- 500g / 1lb granulated sugar
- 1 cup honey
- juice of 1 lemon

1. Cut apples into quarters, and remove stems and blemishes.

2. Roughly chop apples and pop them into a large saucepan. Include skins, core and seeds.

3. Pour in water and add rosemary.

4. Bring to a boil, and then lower heat and gently simmer for 45 minutes.

5. Place cheesecloth over a large bowl.

6. Ladle the apple mixture onto cheesecloth.

7. Suspend cheesecloth over the bowl for 3-4 hours.

8. Pop a saucer in the freezer.

9. Measure the liquid in the bowl and pour into a saucepan. For every 500ml, add 250g of sugar, 150g honey and the juice of 1 lemon.

10. Bring to a boil, giving it a good stir and making sure all the sugar is dissolved before it reaches boiling point.

11. Boil for 10 minutes, and then turn off heat.

12. Drop a teaspoon of the liquid onto the cold saucer and pop it in the fridge for 1 minute.

13. Push the mixture with your finger. If it wrinkles, it has reached setting point. If not, continue to boil and test it every few minutes. Make sure to clean the saucer and pop it back into the fridge between

tests—and turn the stove off each time so you don't overcook the jelly. It can take 15 minutes or longer for the jelly to be done.

14. Skim any scum from the surface of the jelly. Turn off heat and allow jelly to rest for 10 minutes.

15. While the jelly is resting, sterilise the jars and lids.

16. Ladle the jelly into the hot sterilised jars, filling them right to the top.

17. Put the lids on immediately.

18. The jelly will set in the jar as it cools.

19. Keep in a cool, dark place. The jelly will last for 1 year.

20. Once opened, keep it in the fridge.

///

IF WE DIDN'T HAVE BEES WE WOULDN'T HAVE THESE !

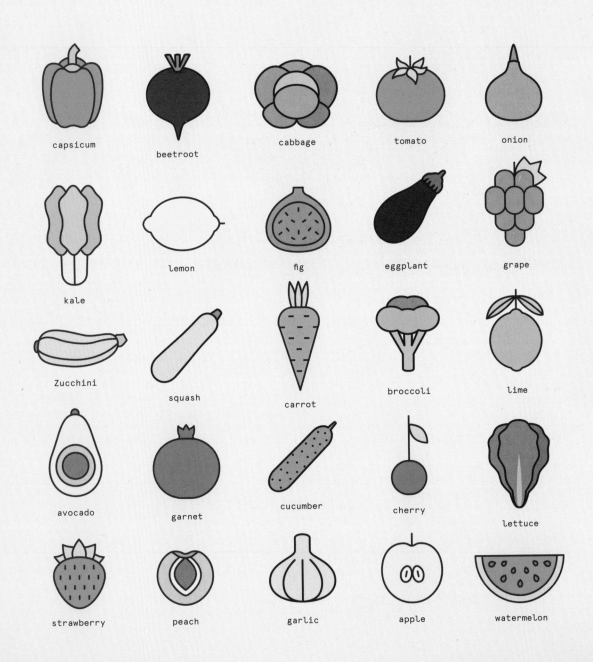

capsicum

beetroot

cabbage

tomato

onion

kale

lemon

fig

eggplant

grape

Zucchini

squash

carrot

broccoli

lime

avocado

garnet

cucumber

cherry

lettuce

strawberry

peach

garlic

apple

watermelon

<<

While honey bees get the most human attention (along with animated movies and marketing deals) because they supply us with sweet food, there are a bunch of wild bees out in nature doing the same basic job of pollinating crops—or sometimes more specific work, because certain plants rely on a single type of bee for survival.

Regardless of whether they're bumblebees or carpenter bees, all bee species have the same basic lifecycle. Inside the hive, there are different casts: there's one individual that lays the eggs—better known as the queen bee—while all the others are worker and drone bees, and their main mission is to collect pollen and nectar, which they transform into honey after returning to the hive.

"What people don't realise is that just in Australia we've got more than 1,600 different species of bees," says Klein. "There's the blue banded bee and the teddy bear bee, which really does look like a teddy bear, but all of them have the same diet. They all rely on pollen and nectar. What's interesting is how we see a co-evolution sometimes, so the plants co-evolve with some species of the bees. There are some nice examples of orchids that have attractive shapes, that look like a bumblebee butt, to attract specific species."

According to Klein, what scientists now know, after studying colony collapse disorder for the last decade, is that numerous factors are to blame, but they can be whittled down to four big ones.

"One of the biggest is that the parasite load of the bee has increased a lot," he says. "Also, pesticides have proven to be very harmful for bees. Environmental damage is known to disturb wild bees specifically, but also honey bees. And climate change, which is actually forcing the plants to change, but then the bees can't adapt quickly enough so we're seeing a trend of disconnection between bees and plants."

Explaining further, Klein points out that the extra parasites that bees are carrying around is due to globalisation, which is our own doing. And yet Klein still manages to see the honey pot as half full. "It's sad, but because it's driven by humans it means we can try and do something to reverse it."

So before you start building a bunker and storing dry foods, the good news is there are lots of things you can do to make your little garden or balcony bee-friendly. Start by buying bee-friendly plants—preferably native ones—that are endemic to your region. Get a hive for the backyard or up on the rooftop of your apartment block. Even if you've got little kids, you can fill the hive with Australian stingless bees, which are perfect for toddlers to keep.

When you're buying honey, it's best to get it direct from your local beekeepers. "If you're interested, I even suggest joining a beekeeper group," says Klein. "It's very good for the bees, the more hives that are around, but also for anyone to be in touch with nature, especially in the city. That's a good way to link back, connect and meet new people."

With the increased popularity of rooftop honey, and beekeeping more generally, it'd be easy to write off the whole movement as a hipster fad, but Klein is passionate when he talks about the importance of each and every beekeeper to the survival of the species. "You keep the stocks up, which helps fight against this collapse that we're seeing at the moment," he explains. "It's also good to have bees to increase the coverage of pollinators in an area. Honey bees can travel up to five or ten kilometres around the hive, collecting. So you never know: the little hive in your little garden could be useful for a local farmer."

Like the insect he fell in love with, Klein travelled a long way from his home in order to learn more. He explains: "Australia is the lucky country when it comes to bees. The population is quite healthy here. When I started studying back in the day, almost six years ago, bees were a hot topic and I quickly realised it was something I wanted to do with my life. I really believe this is something we need to fight for."

///

Bees do the heaviest lifting when it comes to helping plants reproduce all over the world. So it makes sense that we use them to help explain sex; the irony is we're all screwed if they disappear.

busy bodies.

If honey bee colonies were countries they'd be annoyingly smug. They've got it all worked out. Everyone knows their place and everyone is working for the common good. They're basically communists, except each colony has a queen instead of a supreme leader. There is no king. In fact, the queen is pretty much the king and the queen and the entire royal family.

The queen's only job is to make eggs, which become larvae, which become pupae, while the worker bees and drones toil their arses off to make that happen, providing fertilisation, food and wax to construct the hive.

Bees are not troubled by concerns about whether they're in the right career or whether anyone truly values what they do. They are what they are. They work together through pure instinct and they cooperate to survive. I'm not saying I'd like to be a bee. The level of organisation is pretty creepy, and they all wear the same outfit, but you do have to admit: it's all pretty impressive.

Honey bee queens are developed from larvae that have been selected by worker bees and specially fed in order to become sexually mature. There's normally only one adult, mated queen in a hive. Partially because when one 'virgin queen' emerges she wanders around the hive killing any emerging virgin queens she can find.

You might think a queen has it made, but ask yourself this: would you like to give birth all day, every day? That's the queen's gig, and what's worse, even though a healthy queen can produce up to 2,000 eggs in one day, she only gets to do the fun part once. The queen mates a single time early in life (as the only female in a massive bee orgy), after which she stores up millions of sperm within her body.

While a mature queen can live for up to five years (which is Gandalf-standard ancient in insect terms), it often only produces eggs for two or three years, because pumping out thousands of babies every day is exhausting—and not to mention, fairly thankless. When the queen bee gets old and starts to slow down, she is killed by the worker bees she produced, who pile on her, raising her body temperature and causing her to overheat and die. Bless.

DRONE

WORKER

A worker bee's life is short, generally celibate, and filled with hard work and self-sacrifice. They are the unwashed masses of the hive and are, of course, entirely female.

Worker bees pretty much do everything for the hive. They forage for pollen and nectar, tend to queens and drones, feed larvae, ventilate the hive and defend the nest. Their work is never done. If they were humans they'd be working nine to five, doing all the housework, building the actual house, preparing all the food and, on the side, working as vicious kamikaze warriors.

When the hive is attacked, the hard-as-nails worker bees cast off their rubber gloves and charge into battle, using their barbed-stinger arses to defend the colony. Unfortunately, the barbs attach to their victim's skin and tear the stinging bee's abdomen out, which unsurprisingly results in their death.

Don't feel too bad for them, though. The average life span of a worker bee is just six weeks long and, given their lifestyle, that probably seems like more than long enough.

Drones have it made. They are the male honey bees and have only one task in the honey-bee universe: to knock up new queens. High-five! It gets better! These layabout flyboys always mate outdoors and usually in mid-air! Double high-five.

Unfortunately (or fortunately, depending on your point of view), the male fantasy ends here. Shortly after joining the bee equivalent of the mile-high club, before they have the chance to relive their triumph in their tiny bee minds or big-note themselves to their drone friends, they die. That's right: they've reached the mountain top and that's it. Goodbye, stud. Who's next?

Drone bees are considered so generally useless by the rest of the hive (once the queen has been knocked up, that is) that many honey bee colonies will actually eject surviving drones during winter, when food for the colony becomes limited. So not only do these drones not get the chance to pop their clogs mid-air (and remember, that is their only purpose in life) but they are also doomed to wander dateless, hungry and unfulfilled, destined to go out with a plaintive buzz instead of a mid-air bang.

Save the bees by planting these.

hollyhock

sunflower

snowdrop

buttercup

poppy

geranium

borage

THEHORSE

Spring

Time

the grateful

Studies show that grateful kids do better in almost every metric than their non-grateful peers. But how do you even start to cultivate something as ambiguous as gratitude?

Ungrateful: it's one of the parental big guns, the sort of word you reach for when you're being pushed to the edge. But now a growing body of research suggests that cultivating gratitude in your children could be more than just a question of manners. It could also be a way of making your child happier, calmer and able to form stronger relationships. So how exactly do we take our inherently self-centred children and make them care about the outside world? The answer is both simpler and more profound than you might expect.

***

When you're in the day-to-day routine of raising kids, it can be easy to forget how much childhood has changed, even in the space of a single generation. Children today often live lives of exceptional plenty, where the immense benefits of growing up in the well-to-do West happen to them as if by magic. Delicious, healthy food arrives on their plate; entertainment is beamed to their iPad; well-meaning chauffeurs or parents drive them wherever they need. Their bedrooms are cathedrals to various whims and amusements, often expensive and quickly forgotten.

Amanda Miller is the chair of Kids in Philanthropy, a not-for-profit group dedicated to developing gratitude in children by making charity an everyday activity. As she tells me, "It's about trying to help kids recognise that even though their life might be very comfortable and they've got everything they need, there might be kids living only fifteen minutes away who face a very different set of circumstances." For Miller, the light-bulb moment came when she realised that the biggest problem her children had faced in the previous week was when the wi-fi stopped working. "I just started to think that this wasn't the real world—my kids are living in a bubble. How can I expose my children to what's going on out there?"

This certainly isn't a call for a return to a childhood of privation, but gratitude by its very nature requires a sense of one's place in the world, and all too often children are denied the opportunity to develop these perspectives. It's less a question of doing aid work in sub-Saharan Africa than it is re-involving children in the conditions of their day-to-day existence—from cooking to chores to their own education. When they begin to grasp that, they can begin to understand how their way of life might be different to those around them.

While the importance of gratitude in adulthood has been well-documented by researchers, its role in the development of children is less understood. Indeed, prior to 2006 there hadn't been any research on the topic at all. Perhaps gratitude seemed too nebulous a concept at a time when the question of a child's advancement was more and more one to be answered by their school grades. But then came a rash of studies, all of which pointed to the same conclusion: getting children to count their blessings is one of the best things you can do for them.

In one of the most significant bits of research, 221 eleven- and twelve-year-olds were split into two groups. For the next three weeks, one group wrote a daily list of things they were grateful for, while the other group compiled a list of their "hassles". The results were clear: the group who focused on the positives reported significantly higher levels of gratitude, optimism and life satisfaction, as well as diminished rates of negative feeling. They were also more socially inclined and able to offer more emotional support to others. The findings were similar when fourteen- to nineteen-year-olds were asked the same questions: grateful teenagers were more engaged with their community, had better grades, and were less depressed and materialistic.

>>

For Miller, the light-bulb moment came when she realised that the biggest problem her children had faced in the previous week was when the wi-fi stopped working.

Gratitude isn't a question of making superheroes out of your kids. It's about giving them a solid platform from which to make their transition towards adulthood— one built on hope, optimism and a sense of community.

Seven Ways to Practice Gratitude with Kids, by KIP founder Amanda Miller.

3.

Collect loose change and use it to buy a supermarket gift voucher. These are great to give to homeless people as it offers them agency over their food choices. It also gives your child the experience of having a meaningful impact on someone else's life.

6.

Encourage your kids to go through their toys and their books and choose some that they don't want anymore and could donate to charity. If they're given the authority to decide what they want to give away, they'll be more generous and feel better about doing it.

1.

Talk to your kids about social justice issues. Whether you see a story about homelessness on the news or something in the streets, take the opportunity to discuss these issues with them. They're probably already concerned about something and would love the chance to talk about it.

4.

Install three money jars: one for spending, one for saving and one for giving away. If your kid get money from the Tooth Fairy, maybe encourage them to split it so that at least some of it goes to people who need it more than them.

7.

Plan a bake day or garage sale with your kids, help them organise it and then let them decide where the money they've raised should go. It's about facilitating rather than directing their charitable impulses. When they feel like the project is their own, they're more likely to devote time and energy to it and find the execution rewarding.

2.

If they're interested in a social justice issue, suggest that they make a video or write a story about it to share with friends and family. It's a way of not only articulating their sense of right and wrong, but also exercising their creativity in service of something bigger.

5.

Volunteer in the community. It can be hard to find opportunities to do this with younger children, but organisations like Kids in Philanthropy or Kids Giving Back are good places to start.

Of course, this raises the question: how do we create grateful kids? And when do kids even become capable of gratitude? Developmental psychology suggests gratitude is a phenomenon that most children don't fully grasp until they're on the cusp of adolescence. For instance, only one in five six-year-olds will instinctively say "thank you" when given sweets, while it's almost universal by the time a child turns ten.

Yet it's these early days when a child's core behaviours are formed, and evidence suggests that gratitude, like most things, is a skill to be learnt. "Kids at this age are always looking to their parents to work out what to do," says Miller. "If you make gratitude and giving to others part of what the family values and talks about, then your kids are going to grow up thinking that's how things should work." This can take in everything from asking kids to help prepare dinner—a proven way of reducing fussiness—to putting them in charge of household duties or even simply saying "thank you" yourself, when it's warranted. The more autonomy kids build, the more likely they are to understand the work that goes into providing for them, and how lucky they are that it does.

But for Miller the real work starts outside the home—and it's never too early to start trying to grow this awareness in your children. Kids in Philanthropy welcomes children as young as five into its programs. A big focus of their work is on putting kids in situations where they're exposed to a social justice issue, such as homelessness, and then given the capacity to do something about it. "If you empower kids, they get it," Miller says. "Getting them there in the first place can be difficult, but once you have the kids involved they never go back." A typical example is Hangout for the Homeless, when families spend a night sleeping outside on cardboard boxes while also helping to prepare support packs for people who are actually living on the streets.

But all of this requires buy-in from the parents, and that's where a lot of the work goes on. "If kids have ideas about ways they can help, they're going to need their parents to help make that happen. Over the years I've discovered that while there are some kids who are resistant, more often it's the parents who stand in the way." This goes back to the fundamental tenet of teaching gratitude: be as you want your children to be. Basically, if you want your children to say thank you, and mean it, make sure you're doing it too. And if you want them to give back to their community, well, you better be there right by their side. "Something I do love about this kind of work is that you're also raising empathy and awareness in adults, because a lot of parents aren't exposed to these sorts of issues either."

Miller has witnessed the effects of this commitment on her own children, Hannah, Gabe and Zac. "Once they're clicked into this way of thinking, they start to naturally think of other things they can do." For years, instead of asking for presents at their parties, her children began asking for donations instead. "The amazing part of it is that this starts influencing other kids and then suddenly you have all these children competing with each other as to who can raise the most money for their birthday." After taking part in Hangout for the Homeless one year, Hannah staged a blanket donation drive at her school and collected more than one hundred blankets to donate to a local shelter—all with Amanda's assistance, of course. "The beauty of doing it together with your kids is not only that you're doing something as a family, but also that it raises these questions that can lead to really illuminating conversations. Now when we sit around the dinner table, we're not just talking about school or sports. We're able to have these discussions around homelessness and social justice, too."

Gratitude isn't a question of making superheroes out of your kids. It's about giving them a solid platform from which to make their transition towards adulthood—one built on hope, optimism and a sense of community. The psychological benefits of such an approach now seem manifest, but the philosophers have been telling us this stuff for thousands of years: put gratitude out into the world, and you'll be paid back in happiness and success. It's just about taking the abstract and making it real, day to day and year to year, both for yourself and for the people who need it more than you. As Miller sums it up: "If you involve children in meaningful, hands-on activities, it develops empathy by exposing them to experiences outside of their own. But it also makes them happy—and at a time when children's mental health is such an issue, with distancing technology and instant gratification all around, that is something to be treasured."

It's less a question of doing aid work in sub-Saharan Africa than it is re-involving children in the conditions of their day-to-day existence—from cooking to chores to their own education.

///

a matter

of opinion

by
luke
ryan

Being twenty-two when my cancer diagnosis arrived, I had about as much interest in children as I did asphalt, or the finer points of tax law.

On a shelf in a freezer somewhere back in Perth, Western Australia, sits a small canister of me. More specifically, me in the year 2007, at age twenty-two, full of youth, arrogance, and both literal and metaphorical spunk.

This canister represents the last moments of my virility, before six months of chemotherapy rendered my testicles the genital equivalent of a post-apocalyptic wasteland. Whereas your average man might produce somewhere in the vicinity of seventy-five million sperm per ejaculation, these days I'm coughing out around 100,000, half of which are so confused that they may as well have not shown up at all. Wind whistles over the blasted plains of my testes and the huddled survivors look at each other as if to say, "Well, this is new."

Short-term infertility is an expected side effect of chemotherapy in men; long-term, less so. (These effects are often far more damaging for women, for whom fertility preservation is a bit more complicated than simply ejaculating into a cup.) Being twenty-two when my cancer diagnosis arrived, I had about as much interest in children as I did asphalt, or the finer points of tax law. I seem to recall the clinic offering me counselling, but I could not possibly understand why I'd need it. If anything, the news that I'd no longer be able to get anyone pregnant came as a relief. There's that casual-sex disaster area dispensed with. I deposited my sample with about as much care as I usually devote to the act of masturbation—which is to say, none.

But here we are, ten years on. I'll soon turn thirty-two and the wanderlust and freneticism of my twenties recedes ever further into the distance. I married the love of my life a year ago and together we're settling into a gentle, life-affirming domesticity. We recently made our first batch of pickles, which is the kind of sentence that would have caused twenty-two year old Luke to run screaming over the horizon. Yet now homely rhythms trump hedonistic ones. Maybe there's more to life than 5am finishes and the sort of hangovers that Hemingway would have envied?

Children aren't on the immediate agenda, but the steady drumbeat of parenthood is becoming increasingly difficult to ignore. Pregnancy announcements drop with the regularity of artillery shells detonating just over the hills. Not close enough to alarm, but you know it's just a matter of time until one explodes in your face. We watch as acquaintances vanish behind the veil of new parenthood, a suddenly empty space at parties, as if they've been transported to a different plane of existence. I guess in many ways they have.

My wife has polycystic ovary syndrome, so mixed with my sub-par swimmers, having children is going to have to be a decisive act. Put it this way: we've been 'trying' for four years now and still no result. We've watched other couples wrestling with the anxiety and pain and cost of IVF and it doesn't make one hungry to begin the journey. For us, getting pregnant will by necessity be declarative: goodbye to youth, goodbye to freedom, goodbye to all that. Hello incendiary,

agonising, extraordinary unknown. We hope it was worth it. We've jokingly started referring to the point when all our friends might try and get pregnant en masse as the "suicide pact". Well, mostly joking.

My mother had my brother Liam when she was thirty-three and that always seemed like a good benchmark to have. Five years older than me, now it's Liam's turn to enter the breach. Their first is due in December. The artillery shell has landed right in my backyard and it's my brother who has thrown his body onto it. But perhaps this isn't the waiting catastrophe it can seem from the outside. Perhaps a turn from absence to presence, the stop-motion film of a child I love, growing before my eyes, will be all the proof I need. The final prompt to take that canister down from its shelf and see what wonders lie on the other side. I mean, thirty-three is still more than a year away, and unknown is just another word for the adventure not yet had.

///

by edmund burke

The space underneath my house is fitted out like a low-rent nuclear shelter or an Anaconda store a few months into the zombie apocalypse.

A six-man canvas tent, a two-man 'pop-up' tent and an ensuite tent snuggle up to a chemical toilet and assorted inflatable mattresses. A butane stove rusts alongside a fold-up table and a wind-up LCD light. Fishing rods lean against my canoe, supporting each other in their redundancy. It's all there, a coiled spring of stuff, ready and waiting for the annual Burke family one-day camping trip!

I love camping. I thought I did, anyway. I'm just waiting for it to happen the way I want it to. I didn't camp as a kid in Ireland and my Australian family seems to be fully urbanised. When I suggest a camping trip to my wife, she mutters something about her dodgy lower back before either changing the subject or disappearing for a few hours. Apparently sleeping in a confined space with a sweaty Irishman and two impressively flatulent young boys does not appeal to her.

For me, camping is a bit like my belief that one summer I will get a suntan, despite all the evidence to the contrary. Each year when my skin grows back, the illusion always returns. I dream of crisp summer evenings around a campfire, eating something meaty on a stick. Telling stories to my happy children, planning the next day's fishing or bushwalk and looking forward to an uninterrupted night's rest, lulled to sleep by the gentle breathing of my children and the peaceful rhythm of nature.

The reality is hours packing, hours driving, hours unpacking and hours putting up the tent. Christ, I hate putting up my tent. It never gets easy. No matter how many times I put it up, my mind seems to block out the entire traumatic memory before the next time I put it up. I never learn the 'trick', the knack of putting it up. Or if I do I forget it immediately afterwards. It's groundhog day every time. The heat, the initial attempts to calmly follow the instructions, the slow then rapid descent into Basil Fawlty-style madness. Inevitably I become a sweaty, cursing, breakdancing Tasmanian devil encased in green canvas while the kids look on bemused, asking for snacks and poppers.

Once our shelter is erected, the kids run inside and set about knocking it down again. While this vandalism is taking place I inflate our mattresses, which involves using a pump that plugs into the 12-volt outlets in the car. This pump creates a sound that resembles a banshee who's stood on a piece of Lego. Having blown up our bedding and scared the bejesus out of every single living thing within a 10-kilometre radius in the

When I suggest a camping trip to my wife, she mutters something about her dodgy lower back before either changing the subject or disappearing for a few hours.

process, we are ready to … well … what?

All I want to do is sit down, have a drink and stare shell-shocked into the mosquito-sodden twilight. It is unfortunate that, despite the fact it's still a sweltering thirty degrees as the sun goes down, the kids want me to light a fire and cook some sausages. Earlier that day, when the world was young, I promised them I'd do this, so no fire and no buttered bread is not an option.

I brought firelighters, so lighting the fire is not a problem, and I brought firewood, so fuel is not a problem either. What is a problem is that I decided that, rather than take the packaging of whatever new piece of camping equipment I bought for this trip home with me, I should instead burn it in the fire. The thick black smoke that results palls across the campground like a huge visible fart that can easily be traced back

to me by the other coughing campers who stare menacingly through their watering eyes.

After burning some snags and incinerating a few marshmallows it's time for bed, but not before what resembles a huge rat ventures onto our camp site. The creature, which is around the size of a large cat, is not afraid of us and has obviously made a career of scrounging around for campers' food. My youngest boy is not impressed, grabbing a stick and screaming, "Hey, rat! I think you better stop coming around here or you will be sorry," while my eldest tugs at my arms and says, "Dad, I'm scared. Can I get inside the tent?" I'm scared too—of my youngest boy, who is now running after the rat with his stick, despite the fact that it's roughly the same size as he is.

Internet research will later reveal that the 'rat' is a perfectly harmless brown bandicoot, but I gather up

my own 'wildlife' anyway and we retreat to our tent. I warn the kids not to leave the mesh door open. "If you need to go for a pee, do not leave it open," I warn them sagely with the authority of hard-won experience.

I wake to the whine of mosquitoes around my head and immediately set about squashing the evil fuckers as they groggily enter their happy blood comas on the roof of our tent. By the time the sun finally rises, I have entered a sleep-deprived, mosquito-bitten, itchy psychosis. It's time to go home.

When I eventually get back on the road, I tell myself that next time I'll do it differently, next time it will be better because I do love camping. I'm just waiting for it to happen the way I want it to.

///

by claire alexander johnston

Turns out, this story of motherhood really ages you. A time-travelling red phone box—have a baby and hop inside! The greatest hijack of all time!

I have decided I'm not going to grow old gracefully. I am morally, spiritually and philosophically opposed to it. I'm over thirty, and already three kids deep, so give me the works!

I've been googling lotions and potions and all manner of magical serums. How to meditate for skin elasticity, how to eat for inner youth—I'm so far down the anti-ageing rabbit hole that I've pretty much re-mortgaged the house in order to pay for the truckloads of 'Lypo-Spheric vitamin C', which I'm told is pretty much the elixir of life. Not to mention my subscription to 'Facerobotics': just a little well-placed knuckle rub under your chin, they say, and you'll blast off that turkey neck forever! My neuroses are in full swing. I've spent hours researching the perfect silk pillow to avoid the sleep creases that I'm assured will definitely turn into permanent grooves on my face, like a high-def Google Earth image, all deep ravines and coursing river systems.

If I'm honest, a huge selling point of my recent foray into the world of 'adult braces' was the claim that they help hold up your jaw in older age, to stop your cheekbones caving in. And don't even get me started on my undercrackers. Because I know that it's only a matter of time before my vagina goes grey, my uterus falls out and an army of knitting nannas starts crocheting a bag in which to put away my sex life for good. I even bought a rose quartz fanny wand recently, sold on the magical rejuvenating benefits.

I rang my mother. "This ageing business. I'm not okay with it," I said. "I'm not okay with ANY of it!" She sighed, the long, exasperated sigh of a lifetime spent talking me off a ledge. "Oh my darling, but that's what makes us intriguing and beautiful! As you age, your face tells stories of the life you lived," she says, calmly. (Too calmly, might I add, like my self-esteem isn't about to hurl itself into the abyss.) "But I'm so tired! Kids are so draining! And adult acne is totally a thing!" If my face were a story, it would be the Titanic: eventually they're just scraping rusty old ruins off the seabed, wondering if there's anything left to salvage. And what's the story behind the rogue old-lady skin tags I got while pregnant with both my sons?! ("You know you're pregnant with a boy if you get skin tags!") The sleep-deprived eye bags and the paleness of my skin that's really saying, "This poor bitch has barely slept and has been eating baby leftovers for three days."

Turns out, this story of motherhood really ages you. A time-travelling red phone box—have a baby and hop inside! The greatest hijack of all time! And try as I might, I can't hold back the tide. "But would you really do anything differently?" my mum asks me down the line. Well, YES. For starters, I'd write a letter to my younger vagina! Which would mostly start with "I'm so sorry" and end with "BECAUSE YOU'RE AMAZING!". I poured burning wax on you, plucked, shaved and ignored you. I didn't even realise your true purpose or value, other than I wanted you to look neat and tidy and not make a fuss. I would say, "You, my friend, should get out more! You will never look this good again. Go make love to everyone you meet! (Consensually, and ideally with a condom.)"

To the lines on my face that tell of my lack of silk pillows and the long, broken nights I've had falling asleep upright with a baby in my arms, and/or on top of my face, neck crooked and dribbling into my armpit, I will say, "You, girl, are a badass. You have nurtured your children beautifully. I can see you have laughed a lot with them. And they have felt safe, secure and so very loved tucked under your bingo wings." To my soft tummy, and rounded edges? Your body is the most comforting pillow around. To those boobies that one day I'll be rolling up and tucking into my bra? They fed and nourished three healthy babies. And when it's all done, and I look back on these days, to my darling children, I will say, "You will know how much I loved you, the more I look like roadkill."

///

JOURNEY 42 / INSTORE NOW

OBUS.COM.AU

weavers

allyson rousseau:

"Simple forms, primary colours and an appropriate balance of positive/negative space are all things that I'm constantly aware of, and I find it so satisfying to create with all of those elements in mind."

Can you introduce yourself? Hello! I'm Allyson, a fibre artist and designer based out of Montréal, Québec. I taught myself to weave in late 2013—the final year of my art studies—and have been weaving with increasing devotion ever since. I create all my work out of my home studio, where the boundaries of time, work and life are blurred and melt together as one.

What inspired you to start weaving? I'd come across a feature on fibre artist Mimi Jung, and it was the first time I'd seen someone use weaving to create contemporary fibre art. Something awoke inside me that day, and after I was gifted a small peg lap loom for Christmas, I taught myself to weave.

Do you weave full-time? I do! I would say it's actually full full-time, though, because it's

much more than a nine-to-five, forty-hour-week schedule. It's a lifestyle; it's my life!

How has your style changed over the years? My style has always been my own, but my skill and confidence have improved greatly with each new piece. I have some designs from three years ago that I've re-explored recently, and I feel like there's comfort in knowing that my earlier work is still relevant in some way. I've also become much more comfortable with colour. I went through a phase of black and white only, and slowly started incorporating colour to the point of no return.

What inspires you to create? I find that I take most of my inspiration from the design of everyday life. Simple forms, primary colours and an appropriate balance of positive/ negative space are all things

that I'm constantly aware of, and I find it so satisfying to create with all of those elements in mind. I appreciate the work of (a few) other weavers, but I fully avoid others' work in respect to my own designs. There are so many weavers now, and so many people steal other people's designs, that it makes me feel very protective of my own work. That's something I find very uninspiring, and I try to avoid the internet altogether throughout the working process of a piece.

What do you think about when you're weaving? It depends on what I'm working on. Weaving can demand many different levels of mental energy. If I'm focused on working out the design of something, I'm thinking only of the piece in front of me or other work that might provide a solution to the design issue or idea. If I know the path that

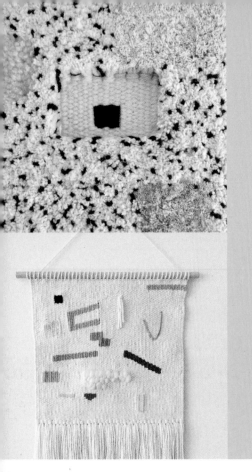

Being a self-employed independent artist requires so much self-motivation and discipline, problem solving, ingenuity, strategy, strength, patience … and you need to be your own cheerleader when everyone else tells you to get a job because being an artist is hard.

a weaving will take, I find my hands can weave independently from my thought and I can be in two places at once. It can be somewhat meditative. And then, of course, I can stream *Seinfeld* on my laptop next to my loom and glance at the screen between weaving lines, which likely means that I'm working on a piece that is very repetitive—for example, weaving 100 lines of the same technique and colour.

What excites you about creating? Creating something that otherwise would not exist. It's such a deeply personal type of work, and it has the artist's touch all over it. Challenging the traditional norms of a medium or craft also excites me and motivates me to grow and push myself as an artist.

What was the last piece you made? A woven necklace for my mum.

What have been the greatest challenges of your art journey so far? Being a self-employed independent artist requires so much self-motivation and discipline, problem solving, ingenuity, strategy, strength, patience—I could go on. It also can be hard to be your own cheerleader when everyone else tells you to get a job because being an artist is hard.

What is success to you? Creating thoughtful work that's original and challenges what already exists. It's me being proud of myself. It's having others recognise my work as being deliberate, and thoughtful, and skilled.

Do you love every piece you make? If I make the effort to follow a piece through to the finish and cut it off the loom, and share it [on the internet], then I think the work is successful. But as time moves forward, my perspective on some work changes. I guess I don't gauge each work by whether I love it or not, but instead by whether I think it is a successful piece, and that is decided by the concept and the overall balance.

What is your work process? I don't spend too much time thinking of design ideas; I let it happen organically. Sometimes I think of an idea as I'm drifting off to sleep, when my mind is the most at peace, or most often when I'm in the middle of creating another weaving. Working

from piece to piece like that tells a lot about my creative process. It shows how one work inspires the next, and ultimately results in designs that are original and genuinely my own.

Did you think that where you are at right now is where you'd end up? I probably always knew that I would be creating and working for myself in some way—as much as I may have fought it for a while. I didn't know that I would be weaving, though. When I was taking studio courses in school I really loved my sculpture class. I had dreams of one day having my own wood shop or ceramic studio and making a living off what I made, but weaving was what naturally stuck and grew and grew and grew. I've been creating soft sculptures

lately that incorporate my woven work, and I'm excited to see where I go with those ideas. I find myself drifting further away from the 2D wall hanging because I'm craving more of a challenge.

What would you say to someone who wants to start weaving but feels intimidated? Just start with the basics and have fun with it. Don't put pressure on yourself to create any one style or master a technique. Experiment! Try stuff out. You will learn so much by teaching yourself through exploration. Don't worry about buying expensive, fancy looms or tools to start: you can do a lot with very little and on the cheap! Most importantly, respect your fellow weavers.

///

genevieve griffiths:

"I made my first weaving in 2012 on a small vintage loom I found in an op-shop. I watched a few tutorials on the internet and then got stuck into making a wild and very wonky weaving."

Can you introduce yourself? I'm an architect by profession but I've always had a great urge to make things with my hands. In recent years, this urge has been largely satisfied with tapestry weaving but I also dabble in ceramics, painting and other more classic mum-crafts, like sewing and knitting.

Describe your family? There is my boyfriend, Jake; my eldest daughter, Sadie, who is two and a half; and our most recent addition, five-month-old baby Pippi.

What were you doing around this time ten years ago? I was living in a sharehouse in inner-city Melbourne, working full-time as a graduate architect and spending all my money on clothes and holidays and going out with friends. (I wouldn't mind a week or two in my old life right now.)

How has your past life intersected with your current life? What skills did you bring with you? Drawing buildings on computers and weaving are pretty different activities, but strangely similar—both deal with linear elements that gradually combine to form a greater whole. Weaving is much more directional than architecture, though, generally starting at one end and moving at a steady pace to the other end (and completion), which I find immensely satisfying compared to the back and forth.

When did you first start weaving? I made my first weaving in 2012 on a small vintage loom that I found in an op-shop. I watched a few tutorials on the internet and then got stuck into making a wild and very wonky weaving. I thoroughly enjoyed the process and was excited by the possibilities of wool as a medium: the colours and textures were seemingly endless. Initially it was a really nice way to spend a few hours on weekends when the urge to get crafty overcame me. It has gradually become much more than that.

Do you weave full-time? Not at the moment, no! With two young girls to look after, I am mumming full-time. I manage to get a bit of weaving done here and there in the daytime, but most of it is done in the evenings when the girls are in bed. It's often the last thing I feel like doing after the exhaustion of the hour-long mind games involved in getting my eldest to sleep, but I always enjoy it once I get started.

What was the last piece you made? I just finished five weavings for an exhibition in Sydney. It nearly killed me.

How did having a child affect your art? There have been ups and downs. I found pregnancy a strangely un-creative time; I kind of hoped that my mind and body would be filled with the glorious miracle of new life and creative energy would pour forth from my loins. But instead all I wanted to do was sit on the couch and eat toast and knit baby clothes. After Sadie was born I slowly got

My partner, Jake, encourages me to loosen up, be more experimental and embrace my mistakes more, but I fear he is fighting a losing battle: my uptight inner architect has a loud voice.

back into weaving, but then we went and had another baby so it all went haywire again. Now that my youngest doesn't need quite so much of my mind/body/soul, I am finding my creative groove again. The kids definitely make me appreciate the time I do get in front of the loom.

What has been the greatest challenge of juggling family and your practice? Apart from simply finding the time to make art, the other big challenge is making sure that the children don't destroy it while I am making it. I don't really have a studio at the moment so I just weave in a corner of the living/dining room—and it is a treacherous location.

Do you love every piece you make? Eventually, yeah, I guess I do. I spend a lot of time with each piece so I really have to love them or it's unbearable. There are always certain parts of the works that I don't like and that bug me, but once the weaving is complete they sort of fade away and it's more about the composition as a whole.

How would you describe your weaving style? It's self-taught Bauhaus modernism.

Where do you draw inspiration from? From endless sources: street signs, modernist art, fabric, Bauhaus architecture, textures in nature, kids' books —and, of course, my archi-tectural background provides a good source of imagery and motifs that recur in my work.

What's been the most chal-lenging part of your weaving journey? Trying to work out

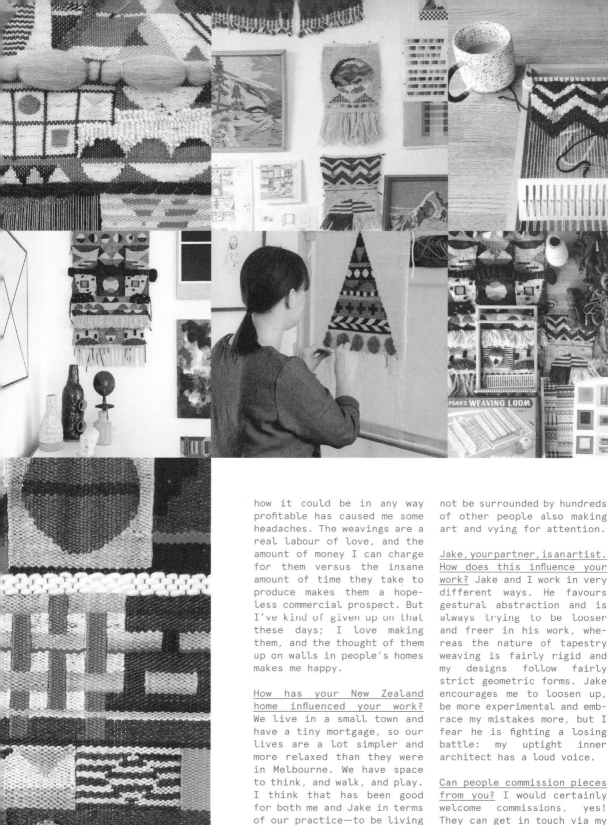

how it could be in any way profitable has caused me some headaches. The weavings are a real labour of love, and the amount of money I can charge for them versus the insane amount of time they take to produce makes them a hopeless commercial prospect. But I've kind of given up on that these days; I love making them, and the thought of them up on walls in people's homes makes me happy.

How has your New Zealand home influenced your work? We live in a small town and have a tiny mortgage, so our lives are a lot simpler and more relaxed than they were in Melbourne. We have space to think, and walk, and play. I think that has been good for both me and Jake in terms of our practice—to be living at a more relaxed pace and to not be surrounded by hundreds of other people also making art and vying for attention.

Jake, your partner, is an artist. How does this influence your work? Jake and I work in very different ways. He favours gestural abstraction and is always trying to be looser and freer in his work, whereas the nature of tapestry weaving is fairly rigid and my designs follow fairly strict geometric forms. Jake encourages me to loosen up, be more experimental and embrace my mistakes more, but I fear he is fighting a losing battle: my uptight inner architect has a loud voice.

Can people commission pieces from you? I would certainly welcome commissions, yes! They can get in touch via my Instagram: @genevievejade. ///

maryanne moodie:

"I love the conversation I have with myself while working on a piece. A combination of meditation and art therapy. Little thoughts bubble up as my hands are busy and I gently allow them to float on by."

What were you doing this time ten years ago? I'd just moved back from living in London and travelling around Europe. I was falling in love with Melbourne again. Teaching art, paying off debts and spending my time reconnecting with family and friends. I met my husband, Aaron, around this time and fell in love.

When did you first pick up a loom? I had burned out from teaching art for ten years and decided to have a baby. While I was cleaning out the store-room, I found an old loom. I rescued it in the hope that it would keep my hands busy while I awaited my babe. I didn't have any yarn at home and just used jute and some waxed cord. I made some swatches of fabric and then hand-sewed little zippers to make coin purses and pencil cases. I gave them out as gifts and it helped me feel reconnected to my friends and family.

What excites you about creating? I love the conversation I have with myself while I'm in the zone working on a piece. A combination of meditation and art therapy. Little thoughts bubble up as my hands are busy and I gently allow them to float on by. The ones that keep popping up help me figure out what conversations I need to be having with myself and my art.

What was the last piece you made? I've recently completed a collection for an exhibition that explored the concept of home and homecoming. We moved back to Australia after living in New York City, and moving was such a lovely, soft moment in our family life. Like a big Aussie hug. Life suddenly felt a lot cleaner, easier and friendlier. The pieces had a real softness and gentleness to them.

Why did you move back to Melbourne from Brooklyn? So that our boys could go to school here. We felt it was important for our kids to grow up identifying as Aussies.

Most of my work, however, remains in the US, so we decided to leave the studio open and running in Brooklyn for the moment. I travel back to the US a few times a year to check in on the studio and teach classes.

Who's in your family? Aaron, my husband, and our two little monsters: Murray, four, and Rudi, two.

How has living in Brooklyn rubbed off on you? Visiting New York is like being tickled, and living in New York can be like being tickled too much. It's awesome and exciting but it can be overwhelming, too. I love the way people in New York are willing to collaborate and connect. Brooklyn was a hive of creative souls and I made some really exciting friendships with lots of very cool folks. It felt like anything was possible!

What's been the greatest challenge of juggling family and

In our family, we're always checking in to see if everyone is happy. If someone is not happy, then we try to change things up until everyone is happy. It's the most important thing.

your growing business? I've never really felt challenged. We have a community of people around our little family who love and support us. We feel very lucky that we have the flexibility to grow and change as needs arise.

Do you still weave every day? YES! Every day. It's still my passion as well as my job. I'm usually working on a few things at once. I recently finished fifteen pieces for an exhibition, two giant pieces for the US Department of State's Art in Embassies program, a collection for a boutique hotel in Barcelona and two private commissions for US clients. I always have three or four looms on the go at the same time.

You have experienced some great press. Can you tell us how this has changed the course of your career? I'm not a planner. When I started weaving, I had no plans other than to weave. The business grew very organically. I was weaving away and making gifts for my mates when Lucy from *The Design Files* happened upon my work. She wrote about me on her blog, which is where Megan Morton found me. She noticed I was a teacher and asked me to teach some classes at The School. I curated kits and a curriculum for teaching weaving. People started to ask if they could purchase the kits and looms, so I worked with a manufacturer to design and make my looms and tools. After that, customers started to ask for a book or an online course, so we produced both of those. I still have no plans. I just like to have my eyes and ears open and listen to my community. It's worked so far!

Do you feel successful? Yes. In our family, we're always checking in to see if everyone is happy. If someone is not happy, then we try to change things up until everyone is happy. It's the most important thing. When I feel happy and my family is happy, I feel successful.

Do you love every piece you make? Yes. They are like little children that I put so much time and thought and energy into.

How long on average does a piece take to make? Usually a few days for an average piece. Sometimes I can work for weeks on a really big, complicated piece.

Do your children influence your work? They influence the amount of time I can spend on my work!

What's been the most challenging part of your weaving journey? I really love my community of weavers and creative women. I used to reply to every comment and really make sure I was connecting with everyone. But a couple of years ago, I realised I was spending too much time locked into Instagram and not enough time connecting with my boys. I'd be pushing them on a swing with one hand and tapping away on Instagram with the other hand. I was not giving either my boys or my business my full attention. So now I read every comment, but I make sure to create a family-work balance. I try to leave my phone in my pocket.

Why did you decide to write a book? My weaving community had been asking for a book. There were lots of complicated vintage books but nothing in current print. Abrams Books approached me and asked if I would consider writing a book on weaving, so I created a list of projects that would both appeal to non-weavers and inspire weavers to get out of their comfort zone and try something new.

You were once a full-time art teacher. Can you tell us a little about that and how that now influences your current job? I loved teaching until I burned out and thought I would never teach again. You would assume that being an art teacher is a creative job, but you spend your whole time trying to inspire creativity in others without nurturing your own inner artist. I was empty by the time I left teaching. But after weaving for a year, I was so passionate about it and my well was overflowing that it made me want to teach again. I love teaching now; it's my favourite part of the job. I get to connect with other weavers and we support and inspire one another.

What would you say to someone who wants to weave but is intimidated because they're a beginner? I have created so many ways for people to feel supported to join the weaving community. Buy my book or join my online course. I sell looms and kits and everything you need. I am a one-stop shop for the weaving-curious.

///

breakfast

pudding

BERRIES, CACAO NIB + TOASTED COCONUT

- 1/2 cup rolled oats or your choice of base
- 1 cup milk of your choice
- 1 tbsp chia seeds
- 1/4 cup blueberries
- 1/2 tsp vanilla extract
- pinch of salt
- honey or your choice of sweetener, to taste
- handful of strawberries, sliced
- 1 tbsp cacao nibs
- toasted coconut flakes, to sprinkle

Place oats, milk, chia seeds, blueberries,
vanilla, salt and sweetener in a bowl and mix
well. Cover and leave overnight. Put oats in a
breakfast bowl and top with strawberries, cacao
nibs and a sprinkle of toasted coconut flakes.

PLUM, DRIED MANGO + MUESLI

· 1/2 cup rolled oats or your choice of base
· 1 cup milk of your choice
· 1 tbsp chia seeds
· 1/2 tsp vanilla extract
· pinch of salt
· honey or your choice of sweetener, to taste
· 2-3 pieces dried mango, sliced
· 1 plum, sliced
· handful of your choice of muesli

Place oats, milk, chia seeds, vanilla,
salt and sweetener in a bowl and mix well.
Cover and leave overnight. Put oats in
a breakfast bowl, top with mango and
plum, and sprinkle with muesli.

PEAR, PISTACHIO + HONEY

- 1/2 cup rolled oats or your choice of base
- 1 cup milk of your choice
- 1 tbsp chia seeds
- 1/4 cup blueberries
- 1/2 tsp vanilla extract
- pinch of salt
- honey or your choice of sweetener, to taste
- 1/2 pear, poached
- 1 tbsp pistachios, crushed
- honey, to drizzle

Place oats, milk, chia seeds, blueberries,
vanilla, salt and sweetener in a bowl and
mix well. Cover and leave overnight. Put oats
in a breakfast bowl, top with poached pear
and pistachios, and drizzle with honey.

GRAPE + POMEGRANATE

- 1/2 cup rolled oats or your choice of base
- 1 cup milk of your choice
- 1 tbsp chia seeds
- 1/2 tsp vanilla extract
- pinch of salt
- honey or your choice of sweetener, to taste
- handful of grapes, sliced
- 1/2 pomegranate
- 1 tbsp bee pollen

Place oats, milk, chia seeds, vanilla,
salt and sweetener in a bowl and mix well.
Cover and leave overnight. Put oats in
a breakfast bowl and top with grapes,
pomegranate and a sprinkle of bee pollen.

Reusable Beeswax Wrap

HONEYBEEWRAP.COM.AU

little

india

LENTIL DHAL

- 2 tbsp coconut oil
- 1 tbsp ground cumin seeds
- 1 tbsp ground coriander seeds
- 3 garlic cloves, chopped
- 1 tin crushed tomatoes
- 2 tbsp ginger, grated
- 1 tbsp ground turmeric
- 2 tsp salt
- 400g / 14oz tin brown lentils
- 1 tin coconut milk
- 250g / 8.8oz cherry tomatoes
- 1 cup coriander, chopped

1. Heat coconut oil in a large pan over medium-high heat.

2. Add cumin and coriander seeds, and toast until they start to brown—about 45 seconds.

3. Add garlic and cook for about 2 minutes.

4. Pop in crushed tomatoes, ginger, turmeric and salt, and cook for 5 minutes, stirring occasionally.

6. Add lentils, coconut milk and cherry tomatoes, and bring back to a simmer.

7. Remove from heat and stir through coriander.

///

NAAN

Makes 8

- 1 tsp sugar
- 1/2 cup warm water
- 2 1/2 tsp active dry yeast
- 2 1/4 cups plain flour
- 1/2 cup natural yogurt
- 1 tbsp oil
- oil, for greasing pan
- 3 tbsp salted butter, melted

1. In the bowl of an electric mixer, add sugar, warm water and yeast.

2. Stir to combine well. Leave for about 10 minutes, until bubbly.

3. Add flour, yoghurt and oil to bowl and, with a dough hook, mix until dough becomes smooth—about 10 minutes.

4. Add a little oil to the sides of the bowl, cover with a damp tea towel and leave the dough to rise in a warm place until it has doubled in size—about 1 hour.

5. Divide dough into 8 equal bits.

6. Roll each bit into a flat circle using a rolling pin.

7. Heat a heavy-based skillet over high heat and lightly grease with oil.

8. Pop the dough on the skillet.

9. When it puffs up and bubbles, flip the dough over and cook the other side.

10. Repeat until done.

11. Brush naan with melted butter. Serve warm.

///

RAITA

- 1 Lebanese cucumber, peeled and thinly sliced
- 1 cup natural yoghurt
- 2 tbsp lemon juice
- 1 tbsp mint, chopped
- pinch of sea salt

1. Pop all ingredients in a bowl and stir together.

2. Cover and refrigerate for at least 3 hours, preferably overnight.

///

SAFFRON RICE

- 2 pinches of saffron threads
- 1 tbsp olive oil
- 1 small onion, finely diced
- 2 cups basmati rice
- 3 3/4 cups stock
- 1 tsp salt

1. Put saffron threads into 1/4 cup of hot water and leave to soak for 5 minutes.

2. While the saffron is soaking, rinse basmati rice in a colander.

3. In a large saucepan, heat olive oil over medium heat, add onion and cook for 10 minutes, until the onion begins to caramelise.

4. Add rice and cook for a minute longer, and then stir onions through the rice.

5. Pour saffron over the rice.

6. Add stock and salt to the pot and bring to a boil.

7. Cover and reduce heat to low. Cook for 20 minutes, or until all the stock is absorbed and the rice is tender.

8. Fluff the rice with a fork before serving.

///

MANGO CHUTNEY

- 1 small onion, peeled and finely chopped
- 1 garlic clove, crushed
- 1 tsp cumin seeds
- 1 tsp yellow mustard seeds
- seeds from 3 cardamom pods
- 1/2 tsp chilli flakes
- 1/2 tsp salt
- 1/2 cup cider vinegar
- 350g / 12.3oz mango flesh, diced
- 1/3 cup caster sugar

1. Pop all ingredients up to and including cider vinegar in a saucepan, and boil until the vinegar has almost evaporated.

2. Add mango and cook until it starts to soften.

3. Add sugar and simmer for 5 minutes, stirring often.

4. Serve straight away or store in the fridge.

///

SAMOSAS

- 2 tbsp vegetable oil
- 1 tsp curry powder, or to taste
- 1 tsp garam masala
- 1/2 tsp ground cumin
- 1/2 tsp ground turmeric
- 1 onion, finely chopped
- 1 garlic clove, finely chopped
- 2 tbsp ginger, grated
- 400g / 14oz tin chickpeas, rinsed and drained
- 200ml / 6.7 fl oz water
- 1/2 tsp sea salt
- 100g / 3.5oz frozen peas, thawed
- juice of 1/2 lemon
- 1 packet of ready-made filo pastry
- 5 tbsp melted butter, for brushing
- 2 tbsp nigella seeds

1. Heat oil in a frying pan over medium-high heat.

2. Add curry powder, garam masala, cumin and turmeric, and cook for 30 seconds.

3. Add onion, garlic and ginger, and cook until onion is soft—about 5 minutes.

4. Pop in chickpeas, and then add water and salt. Cook, stirring, until most of the water has been absorbed. Remove from heat.

5. Stir in peas and lemon juice, and tip into a bowl. Leave to cool completely.

6. Unroll the filo and peel off one sheet. Cover the rest with plastic wrap and a damp tea towel.

7. Lay filo sheet flat on a clean surface and brush with melted butter.

8. Fold in 1/3 of the pastry lengthways towards the middle. Brush again with the butter

and fold in the other side to make a long, triple-layered strip.

9. Place one rounded teaspoon of filling mixture at one end of the strip, leaving a 2cm border. Take the right corner and fold diagonally to the left, enclosing the filling and forming a triangle.

10. Fold again along the upper crease of the triangle. Keep folding in this way until you reach the end of the strip.

11. Brush the samosa with more butter.

12. Pop onto a baking sheet and cover with tea towel while you make the rest.

13. Sprinkle nigella seeds over the top of each samosa.

14. Bake for 30-35 minutes or until golden and crisp, turning halfway through the cooking time.

///

How to Fold a Samosa.

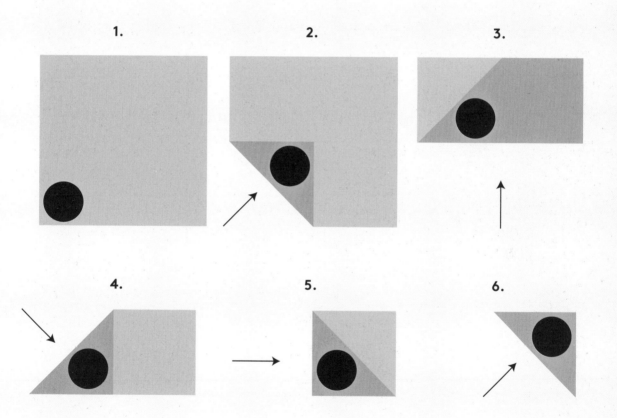

MANGO LASSI

Makes 2

- 1 cup plain yoghurt
- 1/2 cup milk
- 8 ice cubes
- 1 cup ripe mango, chopped
- 4 tsp honey, to taste
- 1/8 tsp ground cardamom
- 1/2 tsp rosewater

1. Pop mango, yoghurt, milk, sugar and cardamom into a food processor and whiz for 2 minutes.

2. Pour into a glass and sprinkle with ground cardamom to serve.

///

ROSE LASSI

Makes 2

- 1 cup plain yoghurt
- 1/2 cup chilled water
- 8 ice cubes
- 1 tsp rosewater
- 2 tbsp rose syrup
- 2 tbsp honey, to taste
- 1 tbsp pistachios, chopped

1. Pop all ingredients, apart from the pistachios, into a food processor and whiz for 2 minutes.

2. Pour into a glass and sprinkle with pistachios to serve.

///

KULFI

<u>Makes 6</u>

- 1/4 cup pistachios, blanched
- 1/4 cup slivered almonds
- 1 cup full-fat milk
- 1 cup double cream
- 3/4 cup condensed milk
- 1/2 tsp ground cardamom
- pistachios for garnish, optional (you can add berries and other fruits, too)

1. Bring a saucepan of water to a boil.

2. Add pistachios to saucepan and simmer for 1 minute.

3. Drain into a colander and rinse with cold water.

4. Pat dry with paper towel.

5. Pop almonds, pistachios and 1/4 cup milk into a food processor and whiz to a smooth paste.

6. Pour into a mixing bowl.

7. Add double cream, remaining milk, condensed milk and cardamom to nut mixture. You can add other fruit at this stage, too. Mix well and adjust the sweetness as needed by adding more condensed milk.

8. Pour into icy-pole moulds and leave in the freezer for 3–4 hours, until set. Add icy-pole stick after 1 hour.

9. After removing the kulfi from the mould, roll in crushed pistachios.

///

ONION BHAJIS

- 3 medium onions, thinly sliced
- 150g / 5.3oz besan flour
- 1/2 tsp baking powder
- 2 tsp ground cumin
- 2 tsp ground coriander
- 1/2 tsp ground turmeric
- 1/2 tsp salt
- 175ml / 5.9 fl oz cold water
- oil, for frying

1. Pop besan flour, baking powder, spices and salt into a mixing bowl. Whisk to combine.

2. Gradually whisk in water to make a smooth batter. Add a little more water if the batter's a little thick.

3. Put onion slices into batter, making sure they're thoroughly coated.

4. Heat about 1cm of oil in a heavy-based frying pan over a medium-high heat. When the oil is hot, place spoonfuls of battered onion into the oil.

5. Cook for 2 minutes, and then turn and cook for another 1-2 minutes, until crisp and golden.

6. Drain on kitchen towel, and serve hot.

///

LIME PICKLE

- 12 limes, cut into quarters
- 150g / 5.2oz sea salt
- 1 tbsp black mustard seeds
- 1 tsp yellow mustard seeds
- 1 tbsp fenugreek seeds
- 1/2 tbsp chilli powder
- 1 tbsp turmeric
- 350ml / 11.8 fl oz extra-virgin olive oil
- 1/2 tsp ground asafoetida

1. In a large bowl, mix the lime quarters with salt.

2. Dry-fry mustard and fenugreek seeds in a small frying pan until fragrant, and then use a mortar and pestle to grind them to powder.

3. Add the ground seeds, turmeric and chilli powder to limes and mix through.

4. Pop limes into a sterilised jar.

5. Heat oil in a pan until it's almost smoking. Add the asafoetida and fry for 30 seconds.

6. Pour the oil over limes in the jar.

7. Place the lid on the jar and keep in a bright place for 2 weeks, shaking the jar daily to distribute the spices.

8. Top up the jar with more oil, if needed.

9. After 2 weeks, store in a cool, dark place. The pickle improves with age.

///

CAULIFLOWER + BROCCOLI PAKORA

- 1 medium cauliflower or broccoli, florets trimmed (you can add any other vegetable you have in the kitchen—we also used green beans)
- 1 cup besan flour
- 1/2 tsp baking powder
- 2 tsp ground cumin
- 2 tsp ground coriander
- 1/2 tsp ground turmeric
- 1/2 tsp salt
- 175ml / 5.9 fl oz cold water
- oil, for frying

1. Pop besan flour, baking powder, spices and salt into a mixing bowl. Whisk to combine.

2. Gradually whisk in water to make a smooth batter. Add a little more water if the batter's a little thick.

3. Pop cauliflower or broccoli florets into the batter, making sure they are thoroughly coated.

4. Heat about 1cm of oil in a heavy-based frying pan over a medium-high heat. When the oil is hot, place spoonfuls of battered veg into the oil.

5. Cook for 2 minutes, and then turn and cook for another 1-2 minutes, until crisp and golden.

6. Drain on kitchen towel, and serve hot.

///

spice,

spice, lady

A BEGINNER'S GUIDE TO BASIC INDIAN SPICES + THEIR BENEFITS

ASAFOETIDA

Asafoetida is a dried resin extracted from the taproot of a flowering perennial herb that is native to Iran and Afghanistan, but it's far more commonly used in Indian dishes. And hold your nose: this is one pungent piece of work.

It goes by quite a few names: *hing, perungayam, jowani badian* and stink finger. Yep, that's right: stink finger. That's what folks called it when Alexander the Great was carrying it around in 400 BC—and that's only mildly less confronting than its French name: *merde du Diable* (devil's shit). Did we mention it smells to high heaven? Yeah, it really does. (That might be why it's also known as 'food of the gods'.) POINT IS, yes, asafoetida *stanks*. It stanks like rotting onions and sulphur and rancid nightmares. But—and please, you gotta trust us on this—it tastes amazing. For real—it brings a totally awesome flavour to your cooking.

Moderation is key: Crush it down from a lump to a powder and add it in tiny quantities to frying oil, cooking stock or water. The harsh aroma will dissipate, leaving behind a strong onion/garlic-like flavour that is particularly well suited to fish and vegetarian dishes. You can also use it

to season pappadums, and some people like to add it to lentil dishes in an effort to … how shall we put this … *reduce flatulence*.

As a traditional medicine, asafoetida has been used to help relieve respiratory conditions like asthma and bronchitis: a chunk of the resin, or a lump of it mixed into a paste, would be hung in a small bag around a sick child's neck. Though whether any relief was due to a true pharmacological effect rather than the sheer physical effort of trying to cough a vile smell out of the lungs remains unclear.

BAY LEAF
(TEZPATTA)

Ahh, the beloved bay leaf. I defy you to find a more controversial 'key ingredient'. Its detractors will tell you that bay leaves are bullshit, that they are little more than flavourless leaf litter, that you could float a strip of old cardboard through your curry instead and none would be the wiser! These people are wrong. The bay leaf is a blessing. You absolutely need it in your kitchen. But, first of all, let's make sure you've got the right one.

There are several varieties of bay leaf out there (all are aromatic laurel leaves). You'll probably be more familiar with the regular European variety, but we're talking about the very different Indian bay leaf, or *Cinnamomum tamala*–which, as the name may suggest, has more of a cinnamon-style flavour.

The Indian bay leaf is also known as *tejpat, tejpatta* (or *tezpatta*), Indian bark, Indian cassia, cinnamon leaf, Malabar leaf and malabathrum. You can easily tell it apart from the more commonly available European products: the Indian bay leaf is much longer and wider, and it has three veins running down it. Indian bay leaves are widely used across India, Nepal and Bhutan, but they're

especially common in North Indian dishes, biryanis and kormas. You'll find the leaves both fresh and dried (and occasionally in powder *form*—but if you can't find them, don't be tempted to substitute with a regular bay leaf, as the flavour profiles are quite different: regular bay leaves have more of a pine/lemon aroma. You're better off using cloves or cassia bark instead.

In medieval times, the leaves were used to produce an ointment, while the ancient Greeks and Romans extracted the fragrant oil for use in perfumes. These days, you pop a leaf or two into your crockpot, pull them out again before serving up, and know that they've made all the difference. Naysayers be damned!

CARDAMOM
(ELAICHI)

Cardamom, or 'the queen of spices', is also known as *cardamome* (French), *cardamomo* (Spanish), *Kardamom* (German) and *cardamone* (Italian). Simple, huh? Sure, but it's *also* also known as *phalazee* (Burmese), *kapulaga* (Indonesian), *elam* (Tamil) and *elaichi* (Indian).

Anyhow, whatever you know it as, just know it's the same thing: the iconic and versatile spice derived from the small seeds of a ginger-like plant.

Cardamom is one of the world's most ancient spices, referenced in some of the earliest Vedic texts. It's native to India and was first traded around the twelfth century from Sri Lanka, but these days it's grown all over the world, most notably in Tanzania and Guatemala. By weight, cardamom is the world's third most expensive spice—just behind vanilla and saffron. Its seeds can either be used whole (keep them in their pods until use to preserve freshness) or split and ground up with other spices for a more diffused flavour. It imparts a warm, lemony-eucalyptus flavour that enhances both sweet and savoury dishes, and pairs especially well with cinnamon and citrus.

Cardamom often features in curries and pilafs, as well as in desserts (you haven't lived until you've tried a rosewater and cardamom custard!) and teas, such as masala chai. The seeds themselves can also be used as a garnish, and were chewed by the ancient Egyptians as a tooth cleaner.

Traditionally, cardamom has been used as a digestive aid to help settle stomachs, just

like ginger. It's also a mild stimulant (not as strong as caffeine) and a *carminative*—that is, something to relieve flatulence (a 'fart-stopper', you might say). Perhaps this explains why Arabs thought it was an aphrodisiac—a reputation that was further cemented by its many references in the stories of the *Arabian Nights*.

CHILLI

Now, no spice rack would be complete without chilli, the fire-powered member of the nightshade family (in fact, a type of capsicum) that originated in Mexico, made its way to South America and then spread throughout the rest of the world. There are literally hundreds of varieties out there, and it's important to know which ones are most appropriate for use in Indian cooking. Some are used for colour, some for flavour and some for their sheer eye-watering heat.

So depending on what sort of meal you're making, you're looking for Kashmiri chilli (not spicy, and more often used as a powder for its red colour), Guntur chilli (very spicy, and used widely in Andhra cuisine), bird's eye chilli (tiny in size, massive in heat, and often used in pickles and chutneys), jwala chilli (the most

popular chilli in India—a light, fruity taste with medium heat, and used fresh and dried), Salem gundu chilli (a uniquely flavoured small, round chilli with lots of seeds and barely any heat, often used in Tamil cooking), Byadagi chilli (less spicy, long and thin, and often dried; imparts more of a paprika flavour and a deep red colour) or naga chilli (this is one of the hottest chillies in the world—we're talking so hot that the Indian army legit wants to 'weaponise' it, so proceed with caution!).

Chillies are hugely beneficial in helping to preserve food, repelling up to 75 per cent of pathogens, which probably explains their immense popularity in parts of the world where refrigeration is uncommon. And there's good evidence that eating lots of spicy food is linked to lower rates of heart disease and longer life spans. While the exact reason for those health benefits hasn't been confirmed, it's thought to be thanks to capsaicin—the chemical that gives chillies their heat. This *can* be problematic for people with stomach ulcers or digestive problems, but for everyone else, the seemingly insane masochism of taking as much heat as you can handle may well pay off.

CINNAMON
(DALCHINI)

Those beautiful curled scrolls of cinnamon sitting in your pantry door have come a long way. They're actually strips of the inner bark of a tropical tree native to Sri Lanka (not to be confused with cassia bark). Even today, the best cinnamon is considered to be from the Sri Lankan coast near Colombo (a region formerly known as Ceylon). It's used in a wide variety of cuisines, and in both sweet and savoury foods. You may find cinnamon called *canela* in European recipes, while it's better known throughout India as *kurundu* (Sinhalese), *karuvappa-dai* (Tamil) or *dalchini* (India).

Its distinctive earthy flavour is thanks to an aromatic essential oil, cinnamaldehyde, which is also what gives it that mild peppery kick on the tongue. Cinnamon sticks can be thrown in whole to flavour a biryani, pilaf or chai tea (just remember to fish them out before serving), while the powder is often used in curries—it's one of the key ingredients in a garam masala spice mix. The sticks are quite difficult to grind down to a fine powder, so unless you have a high-powered spice grinder (a heavy-duty coffee grinder can sometimes do the trick, too) it's probably best to buy cinnamon in powder form. To help preserve flavour, both the sticks and the powder should be stored in an airtight container in a dry, dark, cool place.

In ancient times, cinnamon was more valuable than gold. The Egyptians used it when embalming bodies, and the story goes that the emperor Nero burned a year's supply on his wife's funeral pyre in AD 65. Traditionally, cinnamon has been used to treat bronchitis; as a digestive aid to relieve nausea, diarrhoea and flatulence; and as a means of blood-sugar control for diabetics—but the outcomes of clinical trials have not shown these effects.

CLOVE
(LAUNG)

Cloves—derived from the Latin word for 'nail', *clavus*—are in fact the dried, unopened flower buds of a tree native to Indonesia. We in the Western world are probably most familiar with them holding in cherries or pineapple rings on a Christmas ham or floating around in mulled wine, but their history well outdates us. Archaeologists in Syria found cloves in a ceramic container dating back to around 1700 BC. Early Arab and Chinese traders introduced them to the rest of the world, and today they're cultivated in Brazil, Madagascar, Zanzibar, Sri Lanka and India, where they're also known as *laung*.

Cloves have a warm, woody, peppery profile, and are used in Indian cuisine in pickling spices, chai tea and curries—especially vindaloo, where they feature prominently. For savoury dishes, they're best prepared by sautéing a few whole in oil along with cinnamon sticks, cardamom pods, onion, garlic and ginger (and removing before serving, unless you like the feel of a mouthful of rocks!). In sweeter dishes, they pair particularly well with lemon and sugar, but their powerful flavour can easily dominate a dish, so they're generally used sparingly to impart their characteristic warm, sweet touch. Cloves can quickly lose their flavour once ground up, so if you're using them as a powder, it's best to make it fresh in a coffee grinder and store them whole in a dry, cool container.

Chinese records dating back to 200 BC describe courtiers holding cloves in their mouths to freshen their breath while they addressed an emperor. The buds also contain eugenol, a mild local anaesthetic, which has seen them used as pain relief for toothache (though this isn't considered effective enough by health authorities), and Ayurvedic healers traditionally used cloves to soothe respiratory and digestive ailments.

CORIANDER
(DHANIA)

Coriander (also known in the West as cilantro or Chinese parsley) has been used so widely for so long that historians can't be sure exactly where it came from—though most evidence suggests it originated somewhere in the Middle East. Its seeds (also known as *kotimli*) and its leaves (*dhania*) feature in a wide range of Indian dishes, offering a distinctive flavour that, depending on who you ask, is either "delightfully refreshing, warm and lemony" or "revolting, soapy and reminiscent of crushed bugs"—indeed, the name 'coriander' is thought to be derived from the ancient Greek for 'bed bug'.

introducing the

RAINEBEAU CO.

leak proof **bento style** LUNCH-BOX

DESIGNED IN **AUSTRALIA**

Fills the hungriest of bellies

Order yours today
www.rainebeau.com.au

A genetic variation determines how people perceive the flavour—some people are actually allergic to coriander—so it might be best to check in with your dinner guests before using it too liberally!

If you're cooking with whole seeds, they're best first roasted in a dry pan to help release their aromas and flavours. Ground coriander seeds add a slightly sour, citrusy note to curries, and it's best to crush them up fresh using a mortar and pestle—the coarser they are, the more texture they add to a dish. Coriander is used in garam masala and pairs especially well with cumin, while the South Indian dish sambhar—a lentil-based stew—calls for roasted coriander seeds (called *dhana dal*, and also used as a mouth freshener). Coriander leaves can be used whole as a garnish or finely chopped and mixed through a dish. They do lose their flavour once dried, though, so be sure to always get them fresh.

Traditionally, coriander has been considered an appetiser and a digestive agent—though that might depend on which side of the genetic fence you sit on! It was also once thought to have antiseptic properties, which made it a useful treatment for mouth ulcers.

CUMIN
(ZEERA)

Cumin, coriander's less-controversial sidekick, is an ancient spice native to northern Egypt, where it was used as a spice and as a preservative in the mummification process. It featured heavily in ancient Greek and Roman cuisine, and is frequently mentioned in the Bible as a form of currency used to pay tithes to priests, in both the New and Old testaments. These days, it's grown throughout Africa, China, the Americas and India, and it's widely used in a variety of dishes.

Cumin is the small, dried seed of a type of parsley, and although it tastes quite different from caraway, the two are often confused—partly because the seeds look alike, and partly because the Indian word for cumin, *jeera*, can sometimes *mean* caraway. When in doubt, go with cumin—and note you may also see it called *cheeregum*. Ground cumin imparts an earthy, musky flavour (attributed to the essential oil cuminaldehyde) and can easily be made at home from whole seeds using a mortar and pestle. It's an ideal spice to impart flavour without too much heat, so its ground form features in most Indian curries and is typically included in garam masala, while the whole seeds are often lightly toasted and scattered through basmati rice to add a smoky note and light, nutty texture. In some southern regions of India, the seeds are boiled in water to make a flavoured drink called 'jira water', believed to stimulate metabolism.

Cumin is traditionally considered a digestive aid and treatment for morning sickness, maybe due to its ability to stimulate bile production from the liver—a trait demonstrated in studies with rats but yet to be observed in humans. Other studies have shown that cumin may help control blood sugar for diabetics, but these are yet to be conclusive. Cumin is also a good source of magnesium and iron.

CURRY LEAVES
(CURRY PATTA)

Curry leaves (*meetha neem* or *kari patta*) are about as fundamental as it gets when it comes to Indian cuisine. Depending on the region of your recipe, you'll find them called *bowala* (Punjabi), *karapincha* (Sinhalese), *barsunga* (Bengalese), *kadhi limbu* (Marathi) or *kariveppilai* (Tamil). They're most commonly used in—you guessed it!—curries, particularly throughout south-west India and Sri Lanka, though they can often feature as a flavouring in drinks, chutneys, samosas, dhals, vegetables, soups (especially *rasam*), breads and sauces. Curry leaves are the key to a good *thoran*—a dry green vegetable and cabbage stir-fry—and *vadas*, a fried snack much like a savoury doughnut. They're native to India, but curry leaves are now cultivated all over the world, including in China, Australia and Nigeria, and they feature in many varieties of Asian cuisine.

They're best sourced fresh for the strongest pine-lemon aroma and tangerine-peel taste (which is thanks to several different essential oils present in the leaf), but they can also be used dried for a milder flavour. Make the most of them by frying them in ghee along with onion as one of the first steps in the cooking process. (As with other leaves, if used whole they should be removed from the dish before serving.) They can also be dry toasted and then finely chopped or ground and mixed through a paste. Curry leaves combine well with mustard seeds, turmeric, coriander, cumin, ginger, garlic, tomato and yoghurt.

There's some evidence that curry leaves contain agents that can slow glucose production and are therefore potentially beneficial for helping to control blood-sugar levels in diabetics. They've also been mixed with buttermilk for use as a laxative to ease constipation, and they're a good source of iron and folic acid.

FENUGREEK
(METHI)

Native to India and southern Europe, fenugreek (also called *methi, venthium* or *uluhaal*) was once a wild plant used as cattle feed and soil fertiliser. Fenugreek seeds were found in Tutankhamun's tomb, and other records show the Romans used it to flavour wine. Now domesticated and cultivated around the world, the leaves and seeds can both be used in cooking, though in Indian cuisine it's most commonly the leaves (fresh or

dried)—the roasted seeds are sometimes added to coffee or tea. A compound called 'soto-lon' is what gives fenugreek its unique bittersweet flavour, which is not unlike burnt sugar with an aftertaste reminiscent of celery.

Fenugreek is predominantly used as a powder in meat curries (especially in vindaloo and some Sri Lankan hot curries), vegetable dishes, dhals and fish dishes, as well as in many pickles and chutneys. It is one of the five spices used in *panch phoron,* a blend used widely in Bangladeshi, eastern Indian and southern Nepalese cuisine. If a curry-paste recipe calls for the seeds, it's best to soak them overnight, because this softens them up and makes them easier to combine with other ingredients. When toasting fenugreek seeds, be careful not to overdo it: they can become bitter with too much direct heat.

Although fenugreek was traditionally used as a digestive aid and an anti-diabetic, these benefits are not supported by modern evidence. In fact, fenugreek is more likely to cause digestive discomfort (especially when consumed in high amounts), and some people are allergic to it (especially those with peanut or chickpea allergies). It can also interfere with diabetic drugs, so it should be consumed with caution by some—though, in the small amounts that cooking calls for, this is unlikely to be a problem.

GARLIC
(LASSAN)

Ahhh, garlic. The international all-rounder—just as crucial to the Indian culinary landscape as it is to every other. This is another staple that's been around so long we can't be quite sure where it started, though most sources agree it was likely somewhere in Asia. According to one Arab legend, it first grew from the Devil's footprint as he left the Garden

of Eden. Records show it was eaten by people building the pyramids in ancient Egypt, and the ancient Greeks and Romans knew it lovingly as 'the stinking rose'. In Indian cuisine you'll most likely see it listed as *lashuna, lassan, sudu-lunu* (Sinhalese) or *vellai poondu* (Tamil).

Large chunks of garlic are sometimes used in raitas and pickles, but more commonly you'll chop it finely into thin slivers (or dice it even more finely into a paste) as one of the first steps in a curry base. Simmer it over a low heat in ghee or oil, along with onion and ginger. Be careful not to brown it too much, because when it's overdone the flavour can turn bitter; you're looking to turn the pieces into a near-translucent white. Generally speaking, the slower that garlic is cooked, the more its pungent sweetness is brought out. Dried garlic flakes (you can make these yourself by roasting thinly sliced fresh cloves at a low heat) can sometimes be ground up and used as a powder spice in curries, while small pieces can be added to naan bread for additional flavour.

Widely used in traditional medicine in many cultures, garlic is seen as virtually a cure-all, promising to help with blood pressure, cardiovascular health, digestion, and especially cold and flu—though modern evidence is insufficient to support these claims.

GINGER
(ADRAK)

Ginger gets its (English) name from the Sanskrit word *stringa-vera*, meaning 'body like a horn'—a reference to its gnarled, antler-like shape. Although ginger is often thought of as a root, it is technically a rhizome, which is more like an underground stem. Native to India and China, ginger has long been used as a staple in those cuisines, and at one point it was so popular in Europe that it was included at table settings alongside salt and pepper as a basic seasoning.

Indian recipes will call for the fresh, zesty addition of ginger in pickles, chutneys, curry pastes and curry powders; you may see it called *adruk* (fresh) or *sonth* (dried, powder form). Fresh ginger is often sautéed in oil with garlic and onion to make a paste that forms the flavour basis of many dishes; adding a little salt or vinegar to this paste can help preserve its freshness. Fresh ginger is also used liberally in lentil curries and other vegetable dishes, and juiced for use in both cold and hot drinks, including tea and masala chai. The powdered form is more commonly used in meat curries, such as rogan josh—a Kashmiri special—or murgh kari, the spicy chicken curry.

A number of Indian sweets are also flavoured with crystallised ginger.

Referenced in the *Kama Sutra* as an aphrodisiac, ginger is commonly used as a digestive aid: it's thought to relieve stomach cramps, nausea, motion sickness and indigestion by promoting the secretion of digestive juices and saliva. In medieval times, it was one of the spices used to thwart off the Plague. There's also some suggestion that it could have anti-inflammatory properties and therefore be useful for conditions like arthritis, but the evidence for these effects is unclear.

MUSTARD
(RYE)

Mustard is another global star with a long history and several different varieties. The seeds come from a plant that's part of the Brassicaceae (or Cruciferae) family, meaning it is related to broccoli, brussels sprouts and cabbage. Mustard was a staple spice for the ancient Greeks, and King Louis XI was such a fan of it that he apparently travelled with his own personal supply in a royal pot in case his hosts didn't have any of their own.

In the Indian context you can use yellow, brown or black mustard seeds, but you're ideally

looking for Indian mustard, which is the *Brassica juncea* species. You'll find it called *banarsi rai*, *rayo* or *kimcea*, and more often than not you'll be frying the mustard seeds whole in ghee until they 'pop', releasing a tangy, nutty flavour. Mustard seeds are sometimes ground up with a blend of other spices to make a curry powder (they go very well with cumin, coriander, fennel, curry leaf and asafoetida), while the thick stem of the mustard plant is used to make an Indian pickle called *achar* and a vegetarian Punjabi favourite called *sarson da saag*. Mustard oil (known as *kurva teil*) is also commonly used in North Indian cooking, sometimes as an alternative to ghee.

One of the earliest mentions of mustard for medicinal use is in the Hippocratic writings, where it was recommended for general muscular relief. At various times throughout history it's also been prescribed for scorpion stings, snake bites and toothache, and as an emetic (to induce vomiting). It contains a range of minerals, and the greens are a good source of vitamins A, C and K.

NUTMEG
(JAIPHAL)

First things first: nutmeg is not a nut! So people with nut allergies can rest easy. It is, in fact, the seed kernel found inside the apricot-like fruit of an evergreen tree native to the Moluccas (the 'Spice Islands' of Indonesia) and now cultivated in the West Indies. Nutmeg was first introduced to Europe by Arab traders, and in the Middle Ages it gained a reputation as having magical properties. Records show a monk in the sixteenth century advised young men to carry it around in a vial and "anoint their genitals" with it as a way of ensuring long-lasting virility, while some wore it around their neck as an amulet to ward off evil spirits.

In Indian cuisine it's known as *jaiphal* or *taipmal*, and it's used in both sweet and savoury dishes. Fresh nutmeg is featured heavily in juices, pickles and chutneys from the Kerala Malabar region—where it's believed to have medicinal properties—as well as in Mughlai cuisine, where the warm, sweet, nutty flavour complements the complex blend of other spices. Grated whole nuts are generally preferable in Indian cooking because they impart a fresher, stronger flavour, but nutmeg powder can also be used (and sometimes features in garam masala blends). Note that nutmeg is one of the few spices that should *not* be dry-toasted before blending with other spices, as this can ruin its delicate flavour.

Although nutmeg has been used as a folk medicine for several mostly digestive conditions, it has no proven medical benefit. In fact, nutmeg contains the compound myristicin, which is toxic in high doses and can cause hallucinations and vomiting—but we're talking about levels far higher than you could ever reach in cooking.

PEPPER
(KALI MIRCH)

Pepper, still the world's most traded spice, is known as the 'king of spices' and is sometimes termed 'black gold'. We in the West know it as salt's ubiquitous other half, but it is actually native to South India, where it's known as *kali mirch* and has been part of the flavour profile for thousands of years. It was widespread throughout the ancient world: peppercorns have been found stuffed into the nostrils of Egyptian mummies, and it was a luxury item for the very wealthy in Greece as far back as the fourth century BC. Pepper was a highly valuable commodity in Europe right up until the 1600s, when new trade routes increased supply and helped bring down the price. In Indian cuisine, note that kali mirch always refers to black pepper—that is, the cooked, dried, unripened fruits of the pepper plant (peppercorns), which are usually ground into a powder but sometimes used whole (as opposed to white or green pepper, which is from the same plant but at different stages of processing).

Black pepper should be toasted before blending with other spices, though it can also be ground fresh into a dish towards the end of the cooking process

as a final step of seasoning, to help preserve its spiciness. Sometimes pepper is used in multiple stages of the cooking process—such as in a fiery black pepper chicken curry, which calls for it to be mixed through a meat marinade, toasted in the pan with other ingredients for the sauce and then sprinkled over the meat upon serving. Black pepper's characteristic bite comes from a compound called 'piperine', setting it apart from the capsaicin that gives chilli its fiery flavour.

SAFFRON
(ZAFFRAN/KESAR)

Saffron is one of the world's most expensive spices by weight—and when you learn how it's harvested, you can understand why. It takes around 450,000 hand-picked stigmas (the delicate, rust-coloured threads from the centre of the dried saffron crocus) to make a single kilogram of saffron spice—an entire week's worth of manual labour. By the time it hits a retail shelf, its price is over $5,000 a kilo; fortunately, a little goes a long way.

People have been using saffron for over 3,500 years. It was most likely first cultivated in Persia, but is believed to have originated as a wild variety on the Greek island of Crete. From there it slowly spread through Europe, North Africa and Asia, where it became highly sought after for use as a perfume, dye and medicinal herb. Today, Iran produces 90 per cent of the world's supply. Saffron imparts a strong honey-and-hay aroma with a slightly bittersweet taste, and provides a rich yellow colouring to food—and it's also used as a textile dye. Although saffron can be bought in powdered form, this is very strongly frowned upon as it is often mixed with inferior adulterants.

In cooking, you should always use whole saffron threads, freshly crushed just before use—and generally speaking, the darker, unbroken threads indicate better quality. Just make sure you store them in an airtight container, away from light. In Indian cuisine, saffron is known as *kesa, kesram* or *zafran*, and is often dissolved in hot water or milk for a couple of hours first to steep as much flavour out of the threads as possible. It's added to rice dishes (such as pilafs and biryani) as a colourful festive touch, and to curries and sweets on special occasions—for example, it's an ingredient in the creamy Indian rice pudding dish *kheer*, which is often served during the festival of Diwali or at weddings.

STAR ANISE
(CHAKRA PHOOL)

Star anise originated in Asia—it's long been a staple in Chinese cooking—but it has also featured in Indian cuisine for many hundreds of years (where it's known as *chakra phool*). The spice is in fact the fruit of the *Illicium verum* tree, harvested just before ripening and dried in its star-shaped pod form. (Side note: star anise should not be mistaken for Japanese anise, which is highly toxic and used only as an incense.) As its name suggests, star anise has a distinctive and strong aniseed or liquorice flavour, imparted by the aromatic compound anethole. This is the same chemical that gives regular anise its aniseed flavour, but the two plants are not actually related.

Star anise is used to bring out the flavour of meats, and it's prevalent in Indian staples such as biryani or masala chai. Add a couple of whole pods directly to a pot or grind one down into a powder. The flavour is strong, so use the pods or powder sparingly and taste as you go. You'll also see star anise in sweet dishes, either as a flavouring agent or as a garnish.

Traditionally viewed as a digestive aid, as a means of relieving rheumatism and muscle aches, and as a mild sedative to aid sleep, star anise also contains a chemical that's key to the production of some anti-influenza drugs, and this is what the majority of the world's supply is actually used for. It's also why there's often a shortage during global outbreaks of swine or bird flu.

TURMERIC
(HALDI)

Turmeric is the *other* bright yellow spice, vastly more affordable than saffron, but unfortunately not a suitable substitute in terms of flavour. Turmeric is a native of South-East Asia. Related to ginger, it's also a rhizome (similar to a root) and has been used in India for thousands of years as a dye, herbal medicine and culinary staple. The name 'turmeric' is believed to be derived from the Latin *terra merita*, meaning 'meritorious earth'. In India it's known as *haldi* (Indian), *kaha* (Sinhalese) or *munjal* (Tamil), and it's still used today in Hindu rituals and to dye holy robes.

You'll generally only find turmeric as a powder, after the plant has been harvested, boiled, dried and ground up. Although its musky citrus/ginger flavour is quite mild, it's particularly effective at masking overly fishy odours, so it's often used in seafood dishes—and it pairs with cumin, coriander and mustard quite well. In large quantities, however, it can become bitter. Turmeric is frequently used in Madras curries and Indian sweets, though more as a golden-yellow dye than for taste, and pieces of fresh turmeric are sometimes used in pickles.

Ayurvedic healers have long used the spice to treat a variety of ailments and as an antiseptic ointment. More recently, curcumin—turmeric's main constituent—has gained a reputation as an anti-inflammatory, anti-Alzheimer's and potential anti-cancer agent, but these claims are not supported by clinical-trial findings. There does seem to be a link between a diet high in curries and spices and good health and longevity, though, so it can't hurt to incorporate turmeric (or any of the many other Indian spices) into your cooking repertoire.

///

The Lunch Lady
Marketplace.

Mother Daughter

Mother Daughter luxurious French flax linen bedding is impeccably cut and sewn with love in our coastal Victorian studio.

wearemotherdaughter.com

Paris-Bourke

Paris-Bourke creates board games printed on fabric. Would you like to travel the easy way?

parisbourke.com

Ruck Rover

Little shop, lots of love.
We sell nice things to wear and use.

ruckrover.com.au

Bun Coffee, Byron Bay

We've been roasting organic, fair trade, Australian and sustainably grown coffee in Byron since 2005.

buncoffee.com.au

Fictional Objects

Cotton and linen bed clothes and
accessories designed in Australia
and manufactured responsibly.

fictionalobjects.com

Sunday Supply Co.

Vintage-inspired beach umbrellas with
classic charm and modern finishes.

sundaysupply.co

Farmer Jo

Drool-worthy Sydney made muesli,
granola, bircher and porridge.
It's really fancy.

farmerjo.com.au

Donna Wilson

Handmade and individually designed
knitted textiles, cushions and objects
for the home. Made with love in the UK.

donnawilson.com

BABA GANOUSH

Makes 1 serve of dip

- 1 medium eggplant
- olive oil, to drizzle
- sea salt, to taste
- 1 garlic clove, grated
- juice of 1 lemon
- 2 tbsp tahini

1. Turn the oven griller on medium-high and place a tray up the top.

2. Slice eggplant into 5mm rounds, sprinkle with salt and pop in a colander in the sink to drain excess liquid. Leave for 10 minutes.

3. Pat eggplant dry with some paper towel and place on a baking tray. Drizzle with olive oil and sprinkle with salt.

4. Grill for 5-10 minutes, turning a couple of times until eggplant has softened and is golden brown.

5. Wrap eggplant in foil and leave for 5 minutes.

6. Peel skin from the eggplant. You can leave a little bit on, as it adds some nice colour and flavour.

7. Add eggplant flesh, lemon juice, garlic and tahini to food processor and whiz until creamy.

8. Season with salt to taste.

9. Store in an airtight container in the fridge.

///

ROAST CARROT + CANNELLINI BEAN

Makes 1 serve of dip

- 1 1/2 cups cannellini beans, cooked
- 3 carrots, scrubbed and chopped
- 2 garlic cloves
- 1 tsp cumin seeds
- extra-virgin olive oil
- splash water, to assist mixing
- sea salt, to taste

1. Preheat your oven to 200°C / 400°F / Gas Mark 6.

2. Pop carrots and whole garlic cloves on a baking tray with a big drizzle of olive oil.

3. Sprinkle over cumin seeds and toss to combine.

4. Roast until tender—about 25 minutes, depending on the size of your carrots.

5. Once cooked, place carrots into a food processor along with cannellini beans and a big splash of olive oil. Whiz until smooth. You might need to add a couple of tablespoons of water to help the mixing.

6. Season with salt to taste.

7. Store in an airtight container in the fridge.

///

CASHEW CREAM + CHIVES

Makes 1 serve of dip

- 1 cup raw cashews, soaked for a couple of hours
- 1 tbsp tahini
- juice of 1 fresh lemon, or to taste
- 2 tbsp extra-virgin olive oil
- 1 tsp garlic, minced
- sea salt, to taste

1. Combine soaked cashews, tahini, lemon juice, olive oil and sea salt in a food processor and whiz until smooth and creamy.

2. Season with salt to taste.

3. Store in an airtight container in the fridge.

///

+ crackers !

CRACKERS

Makes 40

- 1 1/2 cups plain flour
- 1 tsp caster sugar
- 1 tsp sea salt
- 2 tbsp olive oil
- 3/4 cup water
- stuff for sprinkling on top (I used black cumin seeds and fennel seeds)

1. Preheat the oven to 230°C / 450°F / Gas Mark 8.

2. In a medium bowl, whisk all the dry ingredients together.

3. Add the oil and water to the flour mixture. Stir until a sticky dough is formed and all flour is incorporated.

4. Sprinkle your bench lightly with flour and pat dough down with your hands.

5. Roll dough out until it's roughly 3mm thick or even thinner.

6. Combine seeds, for topping, in a bowl and sprinkle them over the dough.

7. Pat the seeds into the dough so they don't fall off.

8. Prick dough all over with a fork, to stop the crackers puffing up.

9. With a sharp knife or pizza cutter, cut the dough into crackers.

10. Using a spatula, place crackers onto a baking tray lined with baking paper.

11. Bake for 15 minutes, or until golden brown.

12. Cool crackers on a wire rack.

13. Store in an airtight container.

///

thank you, thank you

CONTRIBUTORS

Alice Alva
Illustration
012, 016, 022,
023, 066, 096-097,
150, 138-139

Alice Oher
Illustration
076

Allyson Rousseau
Photography
108-111

Anna Niestroj
Illustration
019, 022

Beci Orpin
Illustration + Art
037, 038, 084-085,
086-087

Ben Birchall
Words
036-039

Carly Gaebe
Photography
116-119

Claire Alexander Johnston
Words
102-103

Edmund Burke
Words
084-085, 100-101

Erin Davis
Photography
018-019

Genevieve Griffiths
Photography
112-115

Hannah Carpenter
Photography
cover

Jacinta Moore
Styling
072-074, 078-081,
120-125

Jade O'Donahoo
Recipes + Cooking
+ Illustration
028-035, 128-137
140-149, 154-157

Kitiya Palaskas
Recipes
077

Kirsten Drysdale
Words
140-149

Luke Ryan
Words
018-023, 043, 049-055,
092-095, 098-099, 109-119

Maryanne Moodie
Photography
116-119

Rick Bannister
Words
068-071, 080-083

Sabine Timm
Art
040-045

Sally Mason
Photography
022

. . . .

Mr Kitly
Guild of Objects
Craft Victoria
Tableware
120-125

. . . .

AND

Jade + Clancy O'Donahoo
Dana, Mahlie + Leon
Leviston
Michael Critchely
Meredith Forrester
Ian Goldspink
Jen Djula
Maya Rose + Pepper Lou
Kaz + Dallas of
Cottesloe Beach Shack

///

Lunch Lady
is an independent publication.

Publisher
We Print Nice Things
weprintnicethings.com.au

Lunch Ladies
Kate Berry, Lara Burke, Louise Bannister, Nicole Scurrah

Rad helpers
Beci Orpin, Anna Siddans

Say hello
hello@hellolunchlady.com.au

Become an advertiser
office@hellolunchlady.com.au

Become a stockist
shop@hellolunchlady.com.au

Distribute Lunch Lady
office@hellolunchlady.com.au

Collect the series
shop.hellolunchlady.com.au

ISSN / 2205-0817

Lunch Lady prints on FSC certified paper

hellolunchlady.com.au
instagram / @hellolunchlady

//////

LUNCH LADY #9 ON SALE
December 2017